# Daily

**GRADE 3**

# Math Practice

Editorial Development: Marti Beeck
De Gibbs
Copy Editing: Cathy Harber
Art Direction: Cheryl Puckett
Cover Design: Yuki Meyer
Design/Production: Arynne Elfenbein
Susan Lovell
Jessica Onken

EMC 752

**Evan-Moor®**
*Helping Children Learn*

Visit
*teaching-standards.com*
to view a correlation
of this book.
This is a free service.

**Correlated to
Current Standards**

**Congratulations on your purchase of some of the
finest teaching materials in the world.**

*Photocopying the pages in this book
is permitted for <u>single-classroom use only</u>.
Making photocopies for additional classes
or schools is prohibited.*

005

CPSIA: McNaughton & Gunn, Saline, MI USA  [11/2020]

# What's in the New Edition

This 5- to 10-minute daily warm up has been revised and updated to support current grade-specific math skills.

## What's New

**The updated activities focus on:**

- frequent use of graphics and models
- increased development of fluency
- understanding math concepts, number relationships, operations, and processes
- applying math concepts, operations, and procedural skills
- having students contribute and problem-solve at a higher level

***Daily Math Practice* still provides:**

- five short activities that students can complete independently
- a daily warm-up format consisting of computation, a word problem, and activities that apply a variety of math skills and concepts
- practice of grade-level skills and review of previously learned skills

## Current Strategies and Methods

Try these strategies for extending the *Daily Math Practice* warm up to incorporate current math-education methods:

- Include discussions as a regular part of your math lessons. Encourage sharing of multiple strategies and approaches to solving the math problems.
- Invite students to identify patterns, explain concepts, or compare strategies with a partner or in small groups.
- Provide students with a variety of mathematical tools and scratch paper that they can choose from while solving problems.
- Encourage students to check their own answers using a different method, while asking themselves if their answer makes sense.
- Check students' conceptual understanding by giving them the opportunity to discuss mathematical reasoning and procedures used to solve problems.

# What's in *Daily Math Practice*

## Contents

### 36 Weekly Units

#### Days 1 through 4

Half-page activities offer scaffolded practice in grade-specific, standards-based skills. Each day's activity includes 5 math problems.

- 2 computation problems
- 1 word problem
- 2 questions or problems that apply a variety of math concepts

#### Day 5

A full-page activity provides more extensive practice of one or two target skills or reviews essential math concepts.

### Additional Features

#### Scope and Sequence

The chart on pages 4 and 5 lists the skills practiced in the daily activities for each week.

Note that computation and operations are not listed as specific skills because they are a standard part of each day's activities.

#### Answer Key

Shows the answers for each day's activities in reduced-page format. The answer key begins on page 115.

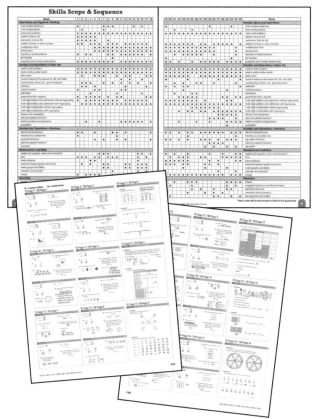

# Skills Scope & Sequence

| Week | 1 | 2 | 3 | 4 | 5 | 6 | 7 | 8 | 9 | 10 | 11 | 12 | 13 | 14 | 15 | 16 | 17 | 18 |
|---|---|---|---|---|---|---|---|---|---|---|---|---|---|---|---|---|---|---|
| **Operations and Algebraic Thinking** | | | | | | | | | | | | | | | | | | |
| write number sentences | ● | | | | | | ● | ● | ● | | | | | ● | | ● | | |
| write word problems | | ● | | | | | ● | | | | | | | | | | | |
| solve word problems | ● | ● | ● | ● | ● | ● | ● | ● | ● | ● | ● | ● | ● | ● | ● | ● | ● | ● |
| addition facts (to 20) | ● | ● | ● | ● | ● | | | | | | | | | | | | | |
| subtraction facts (to 20) | ● | ● | ● | ● | ● | | | ● | | | | | | | | | | |
| addition of three or more numbers | ● | ● | | ● | ● | ● | | | ● | ● | | ● | ● | ● | ● | ● | | |
| multiplication facts | | | | | | ● | ● | ● | ● | ● | ● | ● | ● | ● | ● | ● | ● | ● |
| division facts | | | | | | ● | ● | ● | ● | ● | ● | ● | ● | ● | ● | ● | ● | ● |
| describe or extend patterns | ● | | ● | ● | | | | | ● | ● | | ● | ● | ● | ● | ● | | ● |
| fact families | | | | | | | | | ● | | | | | | | | | |
| properties and number relationships | ● | ● | ● | ● | ● | ● | ● | ● | ● | | ● | ● | ● | ● | ● | ● | ● | ● |
| **Number and Operations in Base Ten** | | | | | | | | | | | | | | | | | | |
| read or write numbers | ● | ● | ● | ● | ● | ● | ● | ● | ● | ● | ● | ● | ● | ● | ● | ● | ● | ● |
| read or write number words | ● | ● | ● | ● | ● | ● | ● | ● | ● | ● | ● | ● | ● | ● | ● | ● | ● | ● |
| place value | | ● | | | ● | ● | ● | | | ● | | ● | ● | | | | ● | ● |
| round numbers to the nearest 10, 100, and 1,000 | | | | | | | | | | | ● | | ● | | | ● | | |
| count by twos, threes, etc., up to thousands | | ● | ● | ● | | | ● | | ● | | ● | | ● | | ● | | | ● |
| odd/even | | ● | ● | | ● | | | | | | ● | | | | | | ● | |
| ordinal numbers | ● | | | | ● | ● | | | | | ● | ● | | | | | | |
| estimation | | | | ● | | | | | | ● | | | | | ● | | | |
| greater/less than, equal to | ● | | ● | ● | ● | | ● | | ● | ● | | | | | | | ● | ● |
| multi-digit addition and subtraction without regrouping | ● | | ● | ● | ● | ● | ● | ● | ● | ● | | ● | ● | ● | ● | ● | | |
| multi-digit addition and subtraction with regrouping | | ● | ● | ● | ● | ● | ● | ● | ● | ● | | ● | ● | ● | ● | ● | ● | ● |
| multi-digit multiplication without regrouping | | | | | | | | | | | | | | | | | | |
| multi-digit multiplication with regrouping | | | | | | | | | | | | | | | | | | |
| division with remainders | | | | | | | | | | | | | | | | | | |
| add and subtract fractions | | | | | | | | | | | | | | | | | | |
| relation symbols and operations | | | ● | | | | ● | | | | ● | ● | ● | ● | ● | ● | | ● |
| probability | | | | | | | | | | | | | | | | | | |
| **Number and Operations—Fractions** | | | | | | | | | | | | | | | | | | |
| identify fractional parts | ● | ● | | | ● | | | | ● | ● | | ● | | | | | | ● |
| fractions on a number line | ● | | | | | | | | | ● | | | | | | | | |
| equivalent fractions | | | | | ● | | ● | | | ● | | ● | | | | | | ● |
| add and subtract fractions | | | | | | | | | | | | | | | | | | |
| decimals | | | | | | | | | | | | | | | | | | |
| **Measurement and Data** | | | | | | | | | | | | | | | | | | |
| weight and capacity: metric (and standard) | | | | | | | ● | ● | ● | | | | | | ● | ● | | ● |
| time | ● | ● | ● | | ● | ● | | ● | ● | ● | | | | | ● | | ● | |
| linear measure | | | | ● | ● | | | | | | | | | | ● | | | |
| read and interpret graphs and charts | | ● | | ● | | | ● | ● | | | | ● | ● | | ● | ● | | |
| create graphs and tables | | | | | | | | ● | ● | | | ● | ● | | ● | ● | ● | |
| calendar and schedule | | | | | | | | | | ● | | | | | ● | | ● | |
| money | ● | | ● | ● | ● | ● | | | ● | ● | ● | ● | ● | ● | ● | ● | ● | ● |
| **Geometry** | | | | | | | | | | | | | | | | | | |
| shapes | | ● | ● | | | | ● | ● | ● | | ● | | | ● | ● | | ● | ● |
| recognize fractions in partitioned shapes | ● | ● | | | ● | ● | ● | | ● | ● | | ● | | | | | | ● |
| perimeter and area | | | | | | ● | | | | | | ● | | | ● | | | |
| symmetry and congruency | | | ● | | | | | | ● | | | | | | | ● | ● | |
| line segments and angles | | | | | | | | | | | | | | | | | | |

| 19 | 20 | 21 | 22 | 23 | 24 | 25 | 26 | 27 | 28 | 29 | 30 | 31 | 32 | 33 | 34 | 35 | 36 | Week |
|---|---|---|---|---|---|---|---|---|---|---|---|---|---|---|---|---|---|---|
| | | | | | | | | | | | | | | | | | | **Number Sense and Operations** |
| ● | | | | | | | | | | ● | | | | | ● | | | write number sentences |
| | | ● | | | ● | | | | | | | | | | | | | write word problems |
| ● | ● | ● | ● | ● | ● | ● | ● | ● | ● | ● | ● | ● | ● | ● | | | ● | solve word problems |
| | | | | | | | | | | | | | | | | | | addition facts (to 20) |
| | | | | | | | | | | | | | | | | | | subtraction facts (to 20) |
| ● | ● | ● | ● | ● | ● | ● | ● | | ● | | ● | ● | ● | ● | | | ● | addition of three or more numbers |
| ● | ● | ● | ● | ● | ● | ● | ● | ● | ● | ● | ● | | | ● | | | | multiplication facts |
| ● | ● | ● | ● | ● | ● | ● | ● | ● | ● | ● | ● | | | ● | | | | division facts |
| | ● | | ● | ● | ● | ● | ● | | | | ● | | | ● | | | | describe or extend patterns |
| ● | | | | | | | | | | | | | | ● | | | | fact families |
| ● | ● | | ● | | ● | | | ● | ● | ● | ● | ● | | ● | ● | ● | ● | properties and number relationships |
| | | | | | | | | | | | | | | | | | | **Number and Operations in Base Ten** |
| ● | ● | ● | ● | ● | ● | ● | ● | ● | ● | ● | ● | ● | ● | ● | ● | ● | ● | read or write numbers |
| ● | ● | ● | ● | ● | ● | ● | ● | ● | ● | ● | ● | ● | ● | ● | ● | ● | ● | read or write number words |
| ● | ● | ● | ● | ● | ● | | ● | ● | ● | ● | ● | ● | ● | ● | ● | ● | ● | place value |
| ● | | | ● | | | | | | | | | ● | | | | | ● | round numbers to the nearest 10, 100, and 1,000 |
| | ● | | ● | | | ● | ● | | | ● | | | | | ● | | | count by twos, threes, etc., up to thousands |
| ● | ● | | ● | ● | | | | | | | | | | | | | ● | odd/even |
| | | | ● | | | | | | | | | | | ● | | | | ordinal numbers |
| | ● | | | | ● | ● | | | | | | | | | | | | estimation |
| | | ● | ● | ● | ● | ● | | | | | | ● | ● | | | ● | ● | greater/less than, equal to |
| ● | ● | ● | ● | ● | ● | ● | ● | | ● | | | | ● | ● | | | | multi-digit addition and subtraction without regrouping |
| ● | ● | ● | ● | ● | ● | ● | ● | ● | ● | ● | ● | ● | ● | ● | ● | ● | ● | multi-digit addition and subtraction with regrouping |
| | | | ● | ● | ● | ● | ● | ● | ● | ● | | | | | | | | multi-digit multiplication without regrouping |
| | | ● | | ● | ● | | ● | ● | | | ● | ● | ● | ● | ● | ● | ● | multi-digit multiplication with regrouping |
| | | | | | | | | | | | ● | ● | ● | ● | ● | | | division with remainders |
| | | | | | | | ● | ● | ● | ● | | | | | ● | | | add and subtract fractions |
| | | ● | | | ● | | | | | ● | | | ● | ● | ● | | ● | relation symbols and operations |
| | | | | | | | | | | | | | | ● | | | | probability |
| | | | | | | | | | | | | | | | | | | **Number and Operations—Fractions** |
| ● | ● | | ● | | ● | ● | | ● | ● | ● | ● | ● | ● | | ● | ● | ● | identify fractional parts |
| | | | ● | | | | | | | | | | | | ● | | | fractions on a number line |
| ● | ● | | ● | | ● | | | ● | ● | ● | | ● | | ● | ● | ● | | equivalent fractions |
| | | | | | | | | ● | ● | ● | ● | | | | | | | add and subtract fractions |
| | | | | | | ● | | | | | ● | | | ● | | ● | | decimals |
| | | | | | | | | | | | | | | | | | | **Measurement and Data** |
| ● | | ● | | | ● | | | | | ● | | ● | | | | ● | ● | weight and capacity: metric (and standard) |
| | ● | | ● | ● | ● | | | ● | ● | | | | ● | ● | ● | ● | ● | time |
| ● | ● | ● | ● | ● | ● | | | | | ● | | ● | | | | ● | ● | linear measure |
| ● | ● | ● | | | ● | | | ● | ● | | | ● | | | | | | read and interpret graphs and charts |
| | | | ● | ● | | | | ● | | | | | | ● | | | | create graphs and tables |
| | | | | | | | | | | | | ● | | | ● | | | calendar and schedule |
| ● | ● | ● | ● | ● | ● | ● | ● | ● | ● | ● | ● | ● | ● | | ● | ● | ● | money |
| | | | | | | | | | | | | | | | | | | **Geometry** |
| | ● | | | ● | ● | ● | | | | | | | | ● | ● | ● | ● | shapes |
| ● | ● | | | ● | | | | | | | | | | ● | | ● | | recognize fractions in partitioned shapes |
| ● | | | | | ● | | | ● | | | ● | | | ● | ● | | | perimeter and area |
| ● | | | ● | | | | ● | | | | ● | | ● | | | | | symmetry and congruency |
| | ● | | | | | | | | | | ● | ● | | | ● | | ● | line segments and angles |

# How to Use *Daily Math Practice*

1. Reproduce the activities for each five-day unit and cut apart the half-page lessons for days 1 through 4.

2. Consult the Scope & Sequence chart (pages 4 and 5) to identify any skills that are unfamiliar to your students. You may want to preview those skills as a whole-class activity.

3. Have students work independently, completing the daily lessons individually, with a partner, or in a small group.

4. Allow sufficient time for sharing solutions and discussing strategies. Modeling a variety of problem-solving techniques offers valuable learning benefits.

**Teaching Tips:**

- Provide students with any tools they need to complete each day's lesson.

- Establish a procedure for students to check their own work.

- Use a day's lesson as a quick, informal assessment.

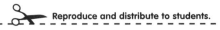 Reproduce and distribute to students.

# How to Solve Word Problems

1. **Read the word problem:** Make a picture of the problem in your mind.
   **Ask yourself:** What is the word problem about?

2. **Think about the problem some more:** Read the problem again.
   Think about the facts or details.
   **Ask yourself:** What do I need to find out?

3. **Draw a picture of the problem:** Draw a part for each number.
   Draw a part for the number you are trying to find.
   **Ask yourself:** What does each number mean?

4. **Solve the problem:** Decide what to do with the numbers.
   **Ask yourself:** What do I need to count, add, or subtract?
   Is there more than one step?

5. **Check your answer:** Write your answer in your picture.
   **Ask yourself:** Does my answer make sense?

1   8 + 12 = _____

    12 + 8 = _____

2   $\begin{array}{r} 9 \\ -\ 3 \\ \hline \square \end{array}$   $\begin{array}{r} \square \\ +\ 3 \\ \hline 9 \end{array}$

3   Write the correct symbol in the circle.

    < = >

4   10 + _____ = 19

    10 + _____ = 20

5   There were 17 girls in Mrs. Baker's class last year. This year there are 9 girls. How many more girls were in Mrs. Baker's class last year?

    _____ girls

1   0 + 10 = _____

    0 + 100 = _____

2   $\begin{array}{r} 13 \\ -\ 6 \\ \hline \square \end{array}$   $\begin{array}{r} 6 \\ +\ \square \\ \hline 13 \end{array}$

3   Color $\frac{1}{8}$.

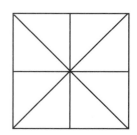

4   Write the number.

    twenty-six    _____

    thirty-three   _____

5   Megan saw a movie about parrots. There were 8 parrots sitting on a branch. Then 6 more landed. Next, 4 flew away. How many parrots were still sitting on the tree?

    _____ parrots

**1**  11 – 7 = _____

   7 + _____ = 11

**2**  $\begin{array}{r} 4 \\ + 9 \\ \hline \square \end{array}$   $\begin{array}{r} \square \\ - 4 \\ \hline 9 \end{array}$

**3**  Mark the eighth dot.

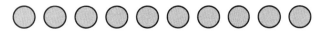

**4**  Count by ones to fill in the missing numbers.

   _____ 100 _____

   _____ 149 _____

   _____ 63 _____

   _____ 102 _____

**5**  If a muffin costs 7¢, how much will 3 muffins cost?

   _____¢

**1**  20 – 6 = _____

**2**  $\begin{array}{r} 5 \\ + 7 \\ \hline \end{array}$   $\begin{array}{r} 7 \\ + 5 \\ \hline \end{array}$

**3**  Continue the pattern.

   11  13  15  _____  _____  _____

**4**  What time is it?   | 9:15 |

   quarter past _____

**5**  Jarod went for a walk on the beach. He saw 9 gulls, 3 cormorants, and 6 pelicans. How many birds did he see altogether?

   _____ birds

## ➤ Activity 1

Complete each number sentence.

Use **3**, **4**, and **5**.

_____ + _____ + _____ = 12

_____ + _____ − _____ = 6

_____ + _____ − _____ = 4

Use **5**, **10**, and **20**.

_____ + _____ + _____ = 35

_____ + _____ − _____ = 25

_____ + _____ − _____ = 15

## ➤ Activity 2

Complete the number lines. Write the missing fractions.

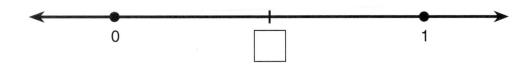

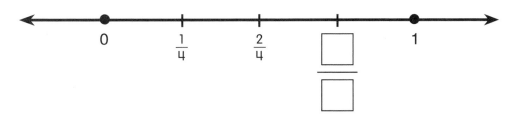

**1** 6 + 7 = _____

_____ − 7 = 6

**2** 11      12
  − 6     − 6

**3** Count by tens.

50 _____ _____ _____ _____

_____ _____ _____ _____ _____

**4** Circle the fraction that names the shaded part.

$\frac{1}{6}$    $\frac{1}{3}$    $\frac{1}{4}$    $\frac{1}{2}$

**5** Tasha practiced her dance for 2 hours before lunch and 3 hours after. How many hours did she practice in all?

_____ hours

**1** 10 − 2 = _____

10 + 2 = _____

**2** 9      19
  + 3    + 3

**3** What time is it?

_____ : _____

**4** 6 + _____ = 15

**5** Write a subtraction word problem for this picture.

_____

_____

_____

_____

1. $18 - 9 =$ _____

   $20 - 10 =$ _____

2.  8          9
   +8         +9
   ___        ___

3. Color the shapes with no corners.

4. Write the number for three hundred.

   _____

5. On Monday, Bob saw 7 deer in the meadow. On Friday, he saw 8 deer. Yesterday, he saw 4 more deer. How many deer did Bob see altogether?

   _____ deer

   Show your work.

1. $9 + 8 =$ _____

   _____ $- 9 = 8$

2.  16         16
   - 4        - 8
   ___        ___

3. Write the numbers in order from least to greatest.

   6     42     17     88     3

   _____ _____ _____ _____ _____

4. If $9 + 5 = 14$, then _____ $- 5 = 9$.

5. Asian elephants can be as tall as 9 feet. African elephants can be as tall as 12 feet. How much taller can African elephants be than Asian elephants?

   _____ feet

## ➤ Activity 1

Mrs. Garcia has been a third-grade teacher at Hillsdale School for 9 years. Mr. Lee taught third grade there for 7 years, and then taught fourth grade for 6 years. How much longer has Mr. Lee been teaching at Hillsdale School than Mrs. Garcia?

Show your work here.

Write your answer here.

_____ years

## ➤ Activity 2

Count. Write the number in the correct column.

|  | Even | Odd |
|---|---|---|
|  |  |  |
|  |  |  |
|  |  |  |
|  |  |  |

**1**   25 + 5 = _____

30 + 5 = _____

**2**   Write **+** or **−** in the circle.

18 ◯ 3 = 15

11 ◯ 4 = 15

**3**   Circle the even numbers.

6      9      12

43      36      65

**4**   thirty − ten = twenty

◯ **yes**      ◯ **no**

**5**   Rainbow stickers cost 10¢ each. How much will it cost Jill to buy 9 stickers?

_____¢

Show your work.

**1**   56 − 5 = _____

**2**
17
+ 9
_____

**3**   Color the rectangle green.
Color the triangle blue.
Color the circle red.

**4**   9 + _____ = 13

13 − 9 = _____

**5**   A mother giraffe is 8 meters tall. Her baby is 3 meters tall. How much taller is the mother giraffe?

_____ meters

**1**   30 + 8 = _____

    32 + 8 = _____

**2**   18          20
     – 6          – 6

**3**

        = _____ ¢

**4**   Write the correct symbol in the circle.

        169 ◯ 183          523 ◯ 299

**5**   Scout Troop 27 went on a trip to a farm. They left at 9:00 a.m. The trip took 2 hours. Mark the clock that shows the time they arrived at the farm.

          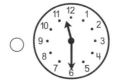

**1**   14 + 3 = _____

    24 + 3 = _____

**2**   20
     – 7
   _____
   ☐          ☐
            + 7
            ____
             20

**3**   Are both sides the same?

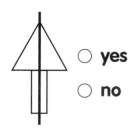

        ◯ yes          ◯ yes

        ◯ no           ◯ no

**4**   Count by twos.

    90 _____ _____ _____ _____ _____

**5**   There are 18 students on Ryan's team. If half are girls, how many boys are on the team?

        _____ boys

➤ **Activity 1**

Follow the lines to make **12** in each direction.

Use these numbers: **1**, **3**, **6**, **7**

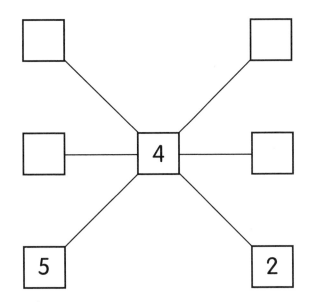

➤ **Activity 2**

Write the missing numbers for each counting pattern.

| twos | 2 | ___ | ___ | 8 | ___ | ___ | ___ | ___ |
|------|---|-----|-----|---|-----|-----|-----|-----|
| threes | 3 | ___ | ___ | ___ | ___ | 18 | ___ | ___ |
| fours | 4 | ___ | 12 | ___ | ___ | ___ | ___ | ___ |
| fives | 5 | ___ | ___ | ___ | ___ | ___ | ___ | 40 |
| sixes | 6 | ___ | ___ | 24 | ___ | ___ | ___ | ___ |
| sevens | 7 | ___ | ___ | ___ | 35 | ___ | ___ | ___ |

**1**   14 – 7 = _____

    24 – 7 = _____

**2**    10        20
    + 4       + 4

**3**   [quarter] + [dime] = _____ ¢

**4**   12 + 6 = 6 + _____

    15 + 5 = 5 + _____

**5**   If pencils cost 10¢ each, how much do 12 pencils cost?

         $_____

Show your work.

**1**   4 + 8 + 2 = _____

    4 + 10 = _____

**2**    20        30
    +10      +10

**3**   Continue the pattern.

 _____ _____ _____ _____

**4**   Circle the sum of twelve + seven = ?

     twenty     nineteen

**5**   Manuel bought 6 toy cars, a kite, and 9 marbles. How many toys did he buy altogether?

       _____ toys

**1**  12 – 2 = _____

22 – 2 = _____

**2**  6      16
+ 5    + 5

**3**  Circle the best estimate for the sum of 98 and 49.

160      140      150

**4**  Continue the pattern.

100  200 _____  _____  _____

**5**  Maya has two cats. Fluffy weighs 3 pounds less than Tigger. If Tigger weighs 9 pounds, how much does Fluffy weigh?

_____ pounds

Show your work.

**1**  18 – 8 = _____

28 – 8 = _____

**2**  7      17
+ 9    + 9

**3**  How long is the crayon?

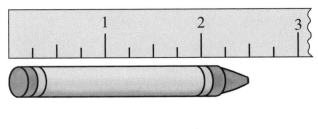

_____ inches

**4**  Write the correct symbol in the circle.

**5**  Jamal rides his bike to school and back home. It is two miles each way. How many miles does he ride in five days?

_____ miles

Look at the graph to answer the questions.

| | Favorite Cookies | | | | |
|---|---|---|---|---|---|
| 14 | | | | | |
| 13 | | | | | |
| 12 | | | | | |
| 11 | | | | | |
| 10 | | | | | |
| 9 | | | | | |
| 8 | | | | | |
| 7 | | | | | |
| 6 | | | | | |
| 5 | | | | | |
| 4 | | | | | |
| 3 | | | | | |
| 2 | | | | | |
| 1 | | | | | |
| 0 | chocolate | chocolate chip | oatmeal | peanut butter | sugar |

**1.** How many different kinds of cookies are named on the graph? _____

**2.** How many kids chose chocolate chip? _____

**3.** Mark the kind of cookie that no one picked.

○ oatmeal

○ peanut butter

○ sugar

**4.** How many kids voted? _____

1  $8 \times 2 =$ _____

   $2 \times 8 =$ _____

2  $\begin{array}{r} 29 \\ -\ 5 \\ \hline \square \end{array}$   $\begin{array}{r} \square \\ +\ 5 \\ \hline 29 \end{array}$

3  Color $\frac{4}{8}$.

4  7 tens and 4 ones = _____

   9 tens and zero ones = _____

5  Evan bought 2 cookies that cost 10¢ each. He gave the clerk a quarter. How much money did Evan get back?

   ○ 5¢    ○ 10¢    ○ 15¢    ○ 20¢

   Show your work.

1  $5 + 8 + 6 =$ _____

2  $3 \times$ _____ $= 9$

   $9 \div 3 =$ _____

3  Circle the ways to make **12**.

   $4 + 8$      $6 + 6$      $13 - 4$

   $5 + 9$      $4 \times 3$      $2 \times 6$

4  Write the missing numbers.

   116 _____ _____ 119 _____ _____

5  Alexa and her parents went on a sailing vacation. It was sunny 9 days of the trip, foggy 2 days, and stormy 3 days. How many days were they on vacation?

   _____ days

1  38 + 21 = _____

2
```
   27            12
 − 12
 ┌────┐       + ┌────┐
 │    │         └────┘
 └────┘          27
```

3  Write the time on the clock.

quarter past 3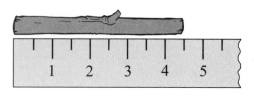

4  Circle the odd numbers.

3     6     9

16    23    54

5  The explorers needed to hike 19 miles in one day. They hiked 8 miles in the morning and 6 miles after lunch. How far did they still need to hike?

_____ miles

Show your work.

1  80 − 4 = _____

90 − 4 = _____

2  5 x 1 = _____        1)5

3  How long is the stick?

_____ cm

4  Write the correct symbol in the circle.

< = >

699 ◯ 966

1,001 ◯ 999

5  A baby elephant is about 3 feet tall when it is born. How much will the elephant have to grow to be 12 feet tall as an adult?

_____ feet

➤ **Activity 1**

1. Draw an **X** on the fifth clown.

2. Circle the eighth clown.

3. Draw a hat on the second clown.

4. Draw a line under the fourth clown.

5. In what position is the last clown?    ○ twentieth    ○ ninth    ○ twelfth

➤ **Activity 2**

Count. Write the number. Then write how many hundreds, tens, and ones.

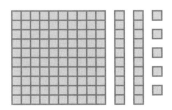

= _____

_____ hundred + _____ tens + _____ ones

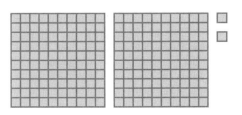

= _____

_____ hundreds + _____ tens + _____ ones

1  $2 \times \underline{\phantom{xx}} = 14$

   $14 \div 2 = \underline{\phantom{xx}}$

2
```
   21        21
   30      +47
  +17      ___
  ___
```

3  What is the perimeter?

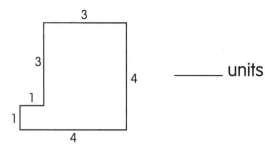

   _____ units

4  Which of these is heaviest?

   ○ car      ○ bus      ○ motorcycle

5  Luis bought a collar, a catnip mouse, and a bag of kitty litter for his new kitten. He gave the clerk $15.00. If Luis got back $3.00 in change, how much did he spend?

   $ _____

   Show your work.

1  $14 + 9 = \underline{\phantom{xx}}$

   $24 + 9 = \underline{\phantom{xx}}$

2
```
   8
  x4
  __
```

3  Circle the amount.

   73¢      68¢      83¢

4  Write **+** or **−** in the circle.

   $17 \bigcirc 9 = 8$

5  The ballgame started at 10:00 a.m. It lasted one and a half hours. At what time did the game end?

   ○ 11:00 a.m.

   ○ 11:30 a.m.

   ○ 11:30 p.m.

1. 16 + 12 = _____

   12 + 16 = _____

2. 
   ```
     30        40
   -  5      -  5
   ```

3. Nine boys, eight girls, and two teachers played ball at recess. How many people in all played ball?

   _____ people

4. Write the number words in the correct order.

   fourth   second   first   third

   _____

   _____

   _____

   _____

5. Which number is one hundred sixteen?

   ○ 161      ○ 160      ○ 116

1. 41 – 9 = _____

2. 
   ```
     18      ┌────┐
   +  7      └────┘
   ┌────┐   -  18
   └────┘    ─────
               7
   ```

3. 
   = _____

4. Write the correct symbol in the circle.

   <   =   >

   2 cups ◯ 1 quart

   2 pints ◯ 1 quart

5. One day, Tanya saw 25 hot-air balloons in the sky. Then 7 of the balloons landed. How many were still in the air?

   _____ hot-air balloons

➤ **Activity 1**

Mom made two large pizzas for Albert and his three friends. Show
how Mom cut the pizzas so that each boy could have three pieces.

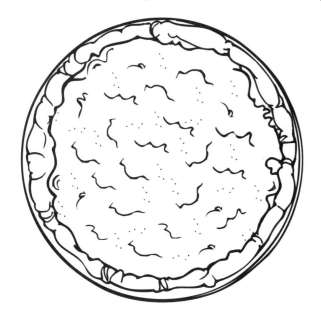
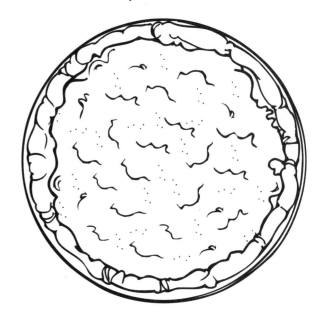

➤ **Activity 2**

How many multiplication facts can you solve in one minute?

| | | | | | | | |
|---|---|---|---|---|---|---|---|
| 2 | 6 | 2 | 4 | 5 | 3 | 2 | 1 |
| x 0 | x 1 | x 3 | x 4 | x 2 | x 3 | x 6 | x 8 |

$4 \times 3 =$ _____      $9 \times 2 =$ _____      $10 \times 4 =$ _____      $7 \times 2 =$ _____

| | | | | | | | |
|---|---|---|---|---|---|---|---|
| 4 | 6 | 8 | 4 | 3 | 9 | 5 | 8 |
| x 5 | x 7 | x 3 | x 6 | x 9 | x 0 | x 7 | x 6 |

_____ correct

**1** $38 - 9 =$ \_\_\_\_\_

$9 +$ \_\_\_\_\_ $= 38$

**2**
$$27 + 10$$     $$37 + 10$$

**3** Draw an **X** on the scale that is used to weigh a person.

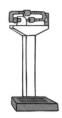  

**4** Count by fives.

75 \_\_\_\_\_ \_\_\_\_\_ \_\_\_\_\_ \_\_\_\_\_ \_\_\_\_\_

**5** If Jo Ellen has 14 socks, how many pairs does she have?

\_\_\_\_\_ pairs

Show your work.

**1** $6 \div 3 =$ \_\_\_\_\_

$3 \times$ \_\_\_\_\_ $= 6$

**2** $5 + 5 + 5 =$ \_\_\_\_\_

$$3 \times 5$$

**3** Congruent figures are exactly the same. Are these shapes congruent?

○ **yes**

○ **no**

**4** Write one less and one more.

\_\_\_\_\_ 420 \_\_\_\_\_

\_\_\_\_\_ 399 \_\_\_\_\_

**5** Write a word problem for the number sentence **2 x 2 = 4**.

_____

_____

_____

_____

1  22 − 10 = _____

   10 + _____ = 22

2  6 x 1 = _____        6 x 2 = _____

   6 x 3 = _____        6 x 4 = _____

3  Write four equations that equal **14**.

   _____        _____

   _____        _____

4  A triangle _____ has three sides.

   ○ sometimes

   ○ never

   ○ always

5  An octopus has eight tentacles. If an octopus wore gloves, how many pairs would it need?

   _____ pairs

1  16 + 9 = _____

   26 + 9 = _____

2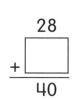
$$\begin{array}{r} 40 \\ -28 \\ \hline \square \end{array} \qquad \begin{array}{r} 28 \\ +\ \square \\ \hline 40 \end{array}$$

3  1 hundred + 6 tens + 9 ones = _____

4  Which unit of measurement would you use to tell how much a bag of apples weighs?

   ○ ounces        ○ pounds

   ○ tons          ○ quarts

5  There are 4 clowns, 3 astronauts, 2 cowboys, and 5 monsters. How many children are at the costume party?

   _____ children

➤ **Activity 1**

Fill in the boxes.

| Cats | | | | | |
|---|---|---|---|---|---|
| | **1** | **2** | **3** | **4** | **5** |
| ears | 2 | | | | |
| legs | 4 | | | | |
| whiskers | 6 | | | | |

➤ **Activity 2**

Jake was very hungry. His mom asked, "Would you like to have $\frac{1}{2}$ of a small pizza, or $\frac{1}{2}$ of an extra large pizza?" Color the choice that gives Jake more to eat.

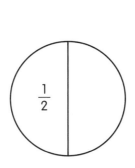
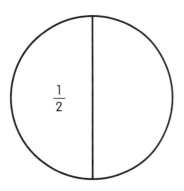

How does the size of the whole pizza make a difference?

_____

_____

_____

**1** $3 \times \underline{\hspace{1cm}} = 12$

$12 \div 3 = \underline{\hspace{1cm}}$

**2**
$$\begin{array}{r} 25 \\ -10 \\ \hline \end{array} \qquad \begin{array}{r} 35 \\ -10 \\ \hline \end{array}$$

**3** Write four equations that equal **15**.

_____  _____

_____  _____

**4** Draw a rectangle.

How many sides?  _____

How many corners?  _____

**5** Mother sent Jessie and Ben to pick corn for dinner. Jessie picked 6 ears. Ben picked twice as many. How many ears of corn did they pick in all?

_____ ears of corn

**1** $16 + 34 = \underline{\hspace{1cm}}$

$\underline{\hspace{1cm}} - 16 = 34$

**2**
$$\begin{array}{r} 32 \\ -10 \\ \hline \end{array} \qquad \begin{array}{r} 42 \\ -10 \\ \hline \end{array}$$

**3** Draw shapes in a repeating AABCC pattern.

\_\_\_\_ \_\_\_\_ \_\_\_\_ \_\_\_\_ \_\_\_\_

\_\_\_\_ \_\_\_\_ \_\_\_\_ \_\_\_\_ \_\_\_\_

**4** What is this number?

two hundred sixteen

○ 20,016    ○ 206    ○ 216

**5** Ellie had twelve pennies. She gave one-fourth of her pennies to Will. How many did she keep?

_____ pennies

**1** 20 + 36 = _____

20 + 58 = _____

**2**
```
  17
–  9
_____
```

**3** Circle the units of measure used to measure water.

gallon        meter        pound

cup        liter        ounce

**4** Write the correct symbol in the circle.

< = >

314 ◯ 304

**5** Jack rode the bus to see his grandma on Saturday. She lives 16 blocks from his house. How many blocks did Jack travel to get there and back?

_____ blocks

**1** 45 – 25 = _____

**2** 3 + 3 + 3 + 3 = _____

3 x 4 = _____

**3** Are the sides symmetrical?

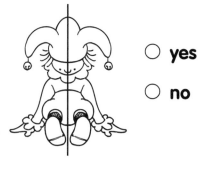

○ **yes**

○ **no**

**4** If 12 + 2 = 14, then 14 – _____ = 12.

**5** Amy made a cake for a family picnic. The cake had to bake for 45 minutes. Amy put it in the oven at 2:00 p.m. Write the time that she took the cake out of the oven.

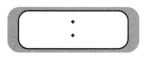

Morgan asked her friends what kinds of pets they have. Record their answers on the graph. Then answer the questions about the graph.

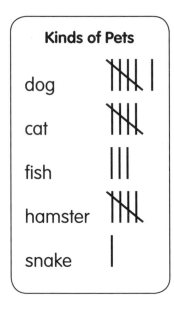

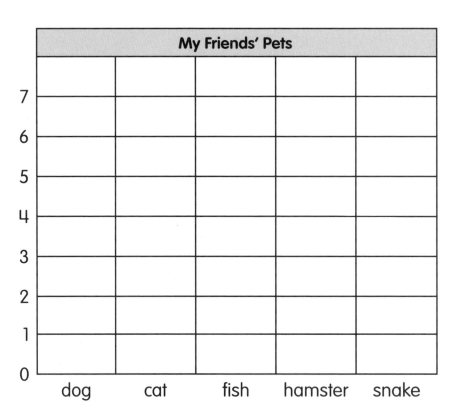

**1.** Which pet did the most people have?

○ dog

○ cat

○ hamster

**2.** Which pet did the fewest people have?

○ fish

○ hamster

○ snake

**1** 6 + 6 + 6 + 6 = _____

6 x 4 = _____

**2**
$$\begin{array}{r} 48 \\ -19 \\ \hline \end{array}$$
☐

$$\begin{array}{r} 19 \\ +\ \square \\ \hline 48 \end{array}$$

**3** Olivia's baby brother Brad weighs 11 pounds. Olivia weighs 77 pounds. What is the difference in their weights?

_____ pounds

**4** If 23 + 7 = 30, then _____ − 7 = 23.

**5** Write number sentences using **7**, **5**, and **12**.

_____ − _____ = _____

_____ − _____ = _____

_____ + _____ = _____

_____ + _____ = _____

**1** 5 x 3 = _____

15 ÷ 5 = _____

**2**
$$\begin{array}{r} 234 \\ +\ 53 \\ \hline \end{array}$$
$$\begin{array}{r} 426 \\ +313 \\ \hline \end{array}$$

**3** Color $\frac{2}{3}$.

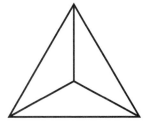

**4** Complete the pattern.

19  23  27  _____  _____  39

**5** Max and James went to the store. It took them 20 minutes to get there, 15 minutes to shop, and 20 minutes to get home. How long were they gone?

_____ minutes

**1** 18 = 3 + 5 + _____

**2**
$$\begin{array}{r} 80 \\ -40 \\ \hline \end{array} \qquad \begin{array}{r} 80 \\ -39 \\ \hline \end{array}$$

**3** Circle the number six hundred three.

63      630      603      6,300

**4** Count by threes.

9  12 _____ _____ _____ _____

**5** Jason had 65¢. He spent a quarter. How much money did he have left?

_____¢

Show your work.

**1** 37 + 54 = _____

**2**
$$\begin{array}{r} 3 \\ \times 6 \\ \hline \end{array}$$

**3** Circle the name of the shape.

rectangle

pentagon

hexagon

**4** 2 x 6 = 6 x _____

3 x 6 = 6 x _____

**5** How many bagels?

$\frac{1}{2}$ dozen = _____ bagels

2 dozen = _____ bagels

Look at the calendar to answer the questions.

| November | | | | | | |
|---|---|---|---|---|---|---|
| **Sun** | **Mon** | **Tues** | **Wed** | **Thurs** | **Fri** | **Sat** |
| | 1 | 2 | 3 | 4 | 5 | 6 |
| 7 | 8 | 9 | 10 | 11 | 12 | 13 |
| 14 | 15 | 16 | 17 | 18 | 19 | 20 |
| 21 | 22 | 23 | 24 | 25 | 26 | 27 |
| 28 | 29 | 30 | | | | |

**1.** What day of the week is November 25?

○ Wednesday    ○ Thursday    ○ Friday

**2.** What day comes after Saturday?

○ Friday    ○ Sunday    ○ Monday

**3.** What is the date of the third Thursday?

○ November 11    ○ November 16    ○ November 18

**4.** What day of the week was October 31?

○ Sunday    ○ Wednesday    ○ Monday

**1** 3 x 3 = _____    5 x 5 = _____

4 x 4 = _____    6 x 6 = _____

**2**
```
  37        47
-  8      -  8
____      ____
```

**3** Draw an **X** on the coins that add up to 45¢.

**4** For each number, circle the digit in the tens place.

29      57      89

**5** Four students brought flowers to their teacher. If each student gave the teacher three flowers, how many flowers did she receive altogether?

_____ flowers

**1** 52 – 18 = _____

**2**
```
  456       329
+ 153      +190
_____      _____
```

**3** Write the number.

thirty-six    _____

fifty-two    _____

**4** Write the time that is 15 minutes later.

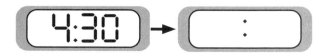

**5** A cook needs a dozen eggs to make an angel food cake. If he has 8 eggs, how many more does he need?

_____ eggs

**1**   60 − 40 = _____

**2**    193        275
    + 26       + 31

**3**   Circle the best estimate for
106 minus 49.

        60     80     100

**4**   Write the correct symbol in the circle.

      <   =   >

    963 ◯ 639

**5**   A cheetah can run 60 miles per hour
for a short distance. A greyhound dog
can run 40 miles per hour. How much
faster can the cheetah run?

     _____ miles per hour

**1**   _____ × 6 = 18

   18 ÷ 6 = _____

**2**    138        742
    + 91       + 83

**3**   eighteen − fifteen = ?

    ◯ two

    ◯ three

    ◯ four

**4**   How much is shaded?

   ◯ $\frac{2}{3}$     ◯ $\frac{1}{2}$     ◯ $\frac{3}{4}$

**5**   If marbles cost 5¢ each, how much
will 6 marbles cost?

     _____¢

➤ **Activity 1**

Mia repaired her old bike. She bought new tires for $20.00, a bell
for $5.00, and a basket for $13.00. How much did she spend?                $_____

If Mia gave the salesclerk $40.00, how much money did she
get back?                                                                   $_____

Show your work.

➤ **Activity 2**

Mark the fraction that is shown as a ● on the number line.

    ○ $\frac{1}{4}$    ○ $\frac{1}{2}$    ○ 1    ○ $\frac{1}{8}$

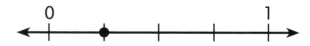    ○ $\frac{1}{4}$    ○ $\frac{1}{2}$    ○ 1    ○ $\frac{1}{8}$

**1** Round 19 to the nearest ten.

○ ten     ○ twenty

**2**
```
   52        74
 – 36      – 25
```

**3** Circle the parallelogram.

**4** If 56 – 32 = 24, then 56 – 24 = _____.

**5** Carnival ride tickets are 10 for $1.00. How many tickets can Keli buy for $4.00?

_____ tickets

Show your work.

**1** 93 – 36 = _____

**2**
```
   52        28
 + 39      + 16
```

**3** Continue the pattern.

400  450  500  _____  _____

_____  _____

**4** Write the correct symbol in the circle.

5 ◯ 7 = 35

**5** Roberto found a sale on canned dog food. Each can cost 40¢. How much did Roberto pay for five cans?

$_____

1. $85 + 7 =$ _____

2. _____ $\times 5 = 35$      $5\overline{)35}$

3. Write the correct symbol in the circle.

    $<$   $=$   $>$

    8 dimes $\bigcirc$ 1 half dollar

    4 quarters $\bigcirc$ 1 dollar

    5 nickels $\bigcirc$ 4 dimes

4. Write **+** or **−** in the circle.

    thirty-five $\bigcirc$ twelve = twenty-three

5. Eight people were on a picnic. Each person drank three cups of lemonade. How many cups of lemonade did they drink altogether?

    _____ cups

    Show your work.

1. $4 \times 7 =$ _____

    $7 \times 4 =$ _____

2. 
    $$\begin{array}{r} 326 \\ -\ 109 \\ \hline \end{array} \qquad \begin{array}{r} 633 \\ -\ 517 \\ \hline \end{array}$$

3. Circle the ways to make **10**.

    $5 \times 2$      $50 - 40$

    $8 + 3$      $20 \div 2$

4. Which ordinal number comes before **sixteenth**?

    ○ fourteenth

    ○ seventeenth

    ○ fifteenth

5. Ian has 15 toy cars. He keeps the cars in 3 boxes. Each box holds the same number of cars. How many cars are in a box?

    _____ cars

➤ **Activity 1**

60 − 20 + 30 + 50 − 40 = _____

Show your work.

100 − 25 + 10 − 35 = _____

Show your work.

➤ **Activity 2**

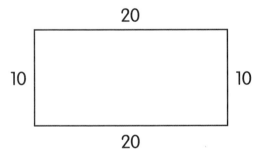

What is the perimeter?

_____ + _____ + _____ + _____ = _____ units

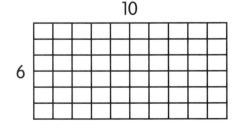

What is the area?

_____ × _____ = _____ square units

1   32 + 52 + 12 = _____

2
```
  534        278
- 380      + 408
```

3   For each number, circle the digit in the tens place. Draw a line under the digit in the ones place.

21      67      83      104

4   Circle the odd numbers.

12      11      15      10      76      81

5   Sara has five brownies. She cut each brownie into fourths. How many pieces does she have?

_____ pieces

1   41 – 29 = _____

2
```
  756        821
+ 223      - 690
```

3   Write the number words in order.

nineteenth      fifteenth      eleventh

_____

_____

_____

4   If 4 x 5 = 20, then 20 ÷ 5 = _____.

5   Today, 67 students are going on a field trip. A bus can hold 50 children. How many buses will be needed?

_____ buses

**1** 5,972 − 0 = _____

**2** 5
  ×6

      6
5)⬚

**3** Color $\frac{3}{8}$.

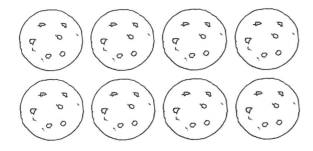

**4** Write the missing numbers.

_____ 257 258 _____ _____ _____

**5** Bananas are on sale. They are 2 for 25¢. How much will 6 bananas cost?

_____¢

Show your work.

**1** 96 − 26 = _____

**2**   65        85
  +25     +15

**3** = _____¢

**4** Write **x** or ÷ in the circle.

28 ◯ 4 = 7

**5** It takes 2 tablespoons (Tbsp.) of peanut butter and 3 teaspoons (tsp.) of jelly to make one sandwich. How much peanut butter and jelly would be needed for 8 sandwiches?

peanut butter = _____ Tbsp.

jelly = _____ tsp.

➤ **Activity 1**

Look at the graph to answer the questions.

**Favorite Foods**

1. Which food do half of the people like best?

_____

2. Which food is the least favorite?

_____

3. Which food do you like best?

○ hamburger

○ taco

○ pizza

○ none of these

➤ **Activity 2**

Solve the word problems.

Randy went out to lunch with his dad. Randy ordered a taco
that cost $2.00. His dad ordered a hamburger that cost
twice as much. How much did the hamburger cost?     $_____

How much did both lunches cost altogether?     $_____

After lunch, Randy and his dad went to see a movie.
Tickets cost $5.00 for a child and $10.00 for an adult.
How much did it cost for both tickets?     $_____

How much did the lunches and the movie cost altogether?     $_____

**1**   58 + 35 + 12 = \_\_\_\_\_

**2**

     ○ 46
     ○ 36
     ○ 30

**3**   Color the cube.

**4**   Continue the pattern.

45   43   41   \_\_\_\_\_   \_\_\_\_\_

\_\_\_\_\_   \_\_\_\_\_   \_\_\_\_\_

**5**   Mia has nine books. One-third of her books are fairy tales. How many of Mia's books are fairy tales?

\_\_\_\_\_ books

**1**   100 − 40 = \_\_\_\_\_

**2**   Round 694 to the nearest 100.

\_\_\_\_\_

**3**   How many?

\_\_\_\_\_ vertices

\_\_\_\_\_ faces

\_\_\_\_\_ edges

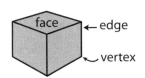

**4**   Count by ones to write the missing numbers.

\_\_\_\_\_ 399 \_\_\_\_\_

\_\_\_\_\_ 600 \_\_\_\_\_

**5**   Jeff was on a bus full of campers. A group of 12 campers got out of the bus while 27 campers stayed inside. How many campers were there in all?

\_\_\_\_\_ campers

**1**　6 x _____ = 24

24 ÷ 6 = _____

**2**　6
　　x 7

　　6)‾7‾

**3**　Tyrone bought two cans of paint. The green paint cost $2.57. The white paint cost $4.35. How much did Tyrone spend altogether?

$_____

**4**

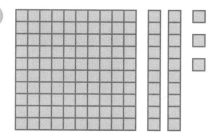

_____ hundred + _____ tens

+ _____ ones = _____

**5**　Mark the number word for **27**.

○ seventy-two

○ seventeen

○ twenty-seven

**1**　88 − 49 = _____

**2**　　792　　　　500
　　+ 133　　　+ 501

**3**　Continue the pattern.

6　12　18　_____　_____

_____　_____

**4**　If 20 + 16 = 36, then 36 − _____ = 20.

**5**　Mei Lee dropped her purse, and her money spilled out. She found 1 quarter, 4 dimes, 3 nickels, and 13 pennies. How much did she find?

_____¢

Show your work.

➤ **Activity 1**

Use the chart to answer the questions.

| Bake Sale | | | |
|---|---|---|---|
| tart | cupcake | brownie | cookie |
| 75¢ | 50¢ | 25¢ | 10¢ |

**1.** How much will two cupcakes and one brownie cost?  $_____

**2.** How much will one tart and four cupcakes cost?  $_____

**3.** How much will one dozen cookies cost?  $_____

➤ **Activity 2**

Write the missing numbers to complete the number sentences.

**1.** If 2 x 3 = _____, then _____ ÷ 3 = 2.

**2.** If 3 x 3 = _____, then _____ ÷ 3 = 3.

**3.** If 4 x 2 = _____, then _____ ÷ 4 = 2.

**4.** If 5 x 3 = _____, then _____ ÷ 3 = 5.

**5.** If 10 x 2 = _____, then _____ ÷ 2 = 10.

**1**  248 + 354 = _____

**2**
```
  736        909
- 255      - 645
```

**3**  Color the trapezoid.

**4**  Continue the pattern.

122  124  _____  _____  _____

**5**  Sienna made a bouquet of flowers for her mother. She used 13 yellow tulips, 12 white carnations, and 6 red roses. How many flowers did Sienna use altogether to make the bouquet?

_____ flowers

---

**1**  7 x _____ = 21

21 ÷ 7 = _____

**2**
```
  659           ☐
- 324        +324
 ☐            659
```

**3**  Draw a repeating ABAC pattern.

_____ _____ _____ _____

_____ _____ _____ _____

**4**  Are these solid figures congruent?

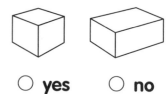

○ **yes**    ○ **no**

**5**  Movie tickets cost $3 for children and $7 for adults. How much will tickets cost for a family of 3 children and 2 adults?

$_____

Daily Math Practice • EMC 752 • © Evan-Moor Corp.

**1** 90 + 40 − 70 = _____

**2**
```
   5        7
 x 7      x 5
```

**3** Circle the butterfly that has a line of symmetry.

**4** If 4 x 9 = 36, then 36 ÷ _____ = 4.

**5** Three third-grade classes are going on a field trip. Two classes each have 28 students and one class has 26 students. How many students altogether are going on the trip?

_____ students

**1** 12,461 − 0 = _____

**2**
```
  436        655
 + 87      + 65
```

**3** one hundred − fifty = ?

○ fifty

○ fifty-five

○ sixty

**4** Write three multiplication facts that equal **24**.

_____ x _____ = 24

_____ x _____ = 24

_____ x _____ = 24

**5** On Saturday, 75 kids went to the beach, but only 48 kids went swimming. How many kids did **not** swim?

_____ kids

> ## Activity 1

1. Shawn and Cody need money for concert tickets. Shawn earned $9.38 walking dogs. Cody earned $6.62 collecting cans and bottles to recycle. How much money do they have so far?

   $_____

2. If they need $18.00 for two tickets, how much more money do they need?

   $_____

> ## Activity 2

Multiply or divide.

| | | |
|---|---|---|
| 2 x 3 = _____ | 6 ÷ 3 = _____ | 3 x 2 = _____ |
| 4 x 2 = _____ | 2 x 4 = _____ | 8 ÷ 2 = _____ |
| 12 ÷ 4 = _____ | 12 ÷ 3 = _____ | 3 x 4 = _____ |
| 3 x 5 = _____ | 5 x 3 = _____ | 3)15 |
| 2)20 | 2 x 10 = _____ | 10 x 2 = _____ |
| 20 ÷ 10 = _____ | 3 x 3 = _____ | 9 ÷ 3 = _____ |

**1** $5 \times$ _____ $= 45$

$45 \div 5 =$ _____

**2**    200          300
      $+600$        $+400$
     _____        _____

**3** Write the missing numbers.

3 hours = _____ minutes

_____ hours = 1 day

_____ months = 2 years

**4** Count by threes.

366  369  _____  _____  _____

_____  _____  _____

**5** David has 26 stuffed animals and Tessa has 39. Which operation would you use to find out how many stuffed animals they have altogether?

○ addition          ○ multiplication
○ subtraction       ○ division

**1** $(18 - 9) \times 4 =$ _____

$9 \times 4 =$ _____

**2**    643          600
      $-471$        $-500$
     _____        _____

**3** Which **two** units could you use to measure juice?

○ centimeters       ○ liters
○ ounces            ○ pounds

**4** Which amount shows where the decimal point belongs in one dollar and twenty-seven cents?

○ $12.7
○ $.127
○ $1.27

**5** There are 3 glasses of water in each one-liter bottle. How many liters in all would 9 people need if they each drank 2 glasses of water?

_____ liters

1  126 − 120 = _____

2  
```
  249
 +460
_____
```
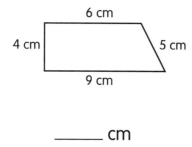
```
 − 249
  460
```

3  Find the perimeter.

6 cm
4 cm
5 cm
9 cm

_____ cm

4  If 4 × 5 = 20, then 5 × _____ = 20.

5  Jasmine baked 2 dozen chocolate chip cookies, 1 dozen oatmeal cookies, and 1 dozen peanut butter cookies for her party. How many cookies did she bake altogether?

○ 48      ○ 40      ○ 36

1  5 × 6 = _____

6 × 5 = _____

2  two hundred + three hundred = ?

○ four hundred
○ five hundred
○ six hundred

3  Mrs. Chang made 137 jars of jam. She sold 93 jars. How many jars does she have left?

_____ jars

4  How many inches are in one foot?

○ 18      ○ 14      ○ 12

5  Are these two shapes congruent?

○ **yes**

○ **no**

Explain why or why not.

_____

_____

_____

➤ **Activity 1**

Make **15** in each direction.

Use these numbers: **1**, **2**, **3**, **5**, **6**

| 8 |   | 4 |
|---|---|---|
|   |   | 9 |
|   | 7 |   |

➤ **Activity 2**

Complete the table.

**Addition Table**

| + | 0 | 1 | 2 | 3 | 4 | 5 | 6 | 7 | 8 | 9 | 10 |
|----|----|----|----|----|----|----|----|----|----|----|----|
| 0 | 0 | 1 | 2 | 3 |   |   |   |   |   |   |    |
| 1 | 1 |   |   |   |   |   | 7 |   |   |   |    |
| 2 | 2 |   |   |   |   | 7 |   |   |   | 11 |    |
| 3 | 3 |   |   |   |   |   |   |   |   |   | 13 |
| 4 |   |   |   |   |   |   |   |   |   |   |    |
| 5 |   |   |   |   |   |   |   |   |   |   |    |
| 6 |   |   | 8 |   |   |   |   |   | 14 |   |    |
| 7 |   |   |   | 11 |   |   |   |   |   |   |    |
| 8 |   |   | 11 |   |   | 14 |   |   |   |   |    |
| 9 |   | 10 |   |   |   |   |   |   |   |   |    |
| 10 |   |   |   |   |   |   |   |   |   | 19 |    |

1. 47 + 40 = _____

   47 + 39 = _____

2. 
$$
\begin{array}{r} 834 \\ -617 \\ \hline \end{array}
\qquad
\begin{array}{r} 742 \\ -328 \\ \hline \end{array}
$$

3. Circle the unit used to measure a person's weight.

   cups    pounds    meters    grams

4. Round each number to the nearest 10.

   49 is almost _____

   21 is almost _____

5. One ice-cream cone costs 48 cents. Draw **X**s on the fewest coins you would use to pay for two ice-cream cones.

1. 7 x 6 = 6 x _____

2. 
$$
\begin{array}{r} 24 \\ 15 \\ 30 \\ +25 \\ \hline \end{array}
\qquad
\begin{array}{r} 12 \\ 50 \\ 44 \\ +31 \\ \hline \end{array}
$$

3. Write **+**, **−**, **x**, or **÷** in the circle.

   63 ◯ 36 = 99

   7 ◯ 8 = 56

4. Color the cylinder.

5. If an elephant eats 200 pounds of food a day, how much will it eat in four days?

   _____ pounds

   Show your work.

52

**1** $25 \div 5 =$ _____

$5 \times$ _____ $= 25$

**2**
$$\begin{array}{r} 8 \\ \times\,7 \\ \hline \end{array} \qquad \begin{array}{r} 7 \\ \times\,8 \\ \hline \end{array}$$

**3** Write four number sentences using **5**, **9**, and **45**.

_____    _____

_____    _____

**4** Circle the best estimate.

$$89 + 67 = ?$$

160     150     170

**5** Mr. Tanaka makes birdhouses. He made 36 blue ones, 24 brown ones, and 16 green ones. How many birdhouses did he make in all?

_____ birdhouses

**1** $124 - 24 =$ _____

**2**
$$\begin{array}{r} 384 \\ +\,169 \\ \hline \end{array} \qquad \begin{array}{r} 426 \\ +\,491 \\ \hline \end{array}$$

**3** Write the numbers below in order from smallest to largest.

29    191    48    196    9

_____ _____ _____ _____ _____

**4** Round each number to the nearest 10.

27 is almost _____

62 is almost _____

118 is almost _____

**5** A bag of peanuts cost Bonnie 65¢. She gave the clerk three quarters. How much change did Bonnie get back?

_____¢

➤ **Activity 1**

Look at each Input and Output number. Figure out the pattern and complete the chart.

What is the rule for the pattern?

_____

_____

_____

| Input | Output |
|-------|--------|
| 4     | 8      |
|       | 18     |
| 12    | 24     |
| 15    |        |
| 20    |        |
|       | 200    |

➤ **Activity 2**

Round to the nearest 10.

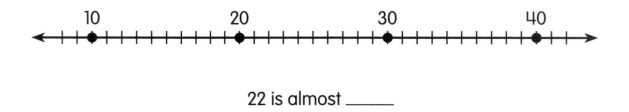

22 is almost _____

87 is almost _____

1　120 – 56 = _____

2　270　　　490
　 +158　　 +204

3　Circle the number two hundred sixty-six.

　　2,066　　266　　626

4　Circle the odd number.

　　72　　63　　92

5　Madison eats 3 pieces of fruit every day. How many days will it take Madison to eat 18 pieces?

　　_____ days

Show your work.

---

1　90 – 63 = _____

2　　3　　　4　　　5
　 × 8　　 × 8　　 × 8

3　Look at the clock. Circle the time that is a half hour later.

　　6:30
　　6:40
　　6:50

4　If 32 + 6 = 38, then _____ – 6 = 32.

5　Arturo has 25 toy dinosaurs. His brother gave him 6 more. How many toy dinosaurs does Arturo have now?

　　_____ toy dinosaurs

Show your work.

**1**   2 x 9 = _____

    9 x 2 = _____

**2**   153        932
  − 27      −271

**3**   Write the expanded number.

    78 = _____ + _____

    92 = _____ + _____

    133 = _____ + _____ + _____

**4**   Write the correct symbol in the circle.

    697 ◯ 796

    895 ◯ 598

**5**   One week has seven days. How many days are in seven weeks?

      _____ days

**1**   32 ÷ 8 = _____

    8 x _____ = 32

**2**   9       9       9
  x 6     x 7     x 8

**3**   Color the cone.

 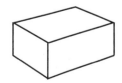 

**4**   Write the correct symbol in the circle.

    3 x 4 ◯ 12 ÷ 3

    4 x 4 ◯ 16 ÷ 4

**5**   Jose had $4.50. He spent $1.42. How much money does Jose have left?

      $_____

➤ **Activity 1**

Look at the schedule to answer the questions.

| Sofia's Schedule | |
|---|---|
| 6:00 a.m.  Wake up | 12:00 p.m.  Lunch |
| 8:00 a.m.  School starts | 3:00 p.m.  School ends |
| 10:30 a.m.  Recess | 5:00 p.m.  Do homework |

**1.** What does Sofia do at 12:00 p.m.? _____

**2.** At what time does Sofia wake up? _____

**3.** How long is Sofia at school? _____ hours

➤ **Activity 2**

Complete the table.

**Multiplication Table**

| x | 1 | 2 | 3 | 4 | 5 | 6 | 7 | 8 | 9 | 10 |
|---|---|---|---|---|---|---|---|---|---|---|
| 1 | 1 | 2 | 3 | | | | | | | |
| 2 | 2 | | | | | | | | | |
| 3 | 3 | | | | | | | | | |
| 4 | | | | 16 | | | | | 36 | |
| 5 | | | | | | 30 | | | | |
| 6 | | 12 | | | | | | | | |
| 7 | | | | | | | | 56 | | |
| 8 | | | 24 | | | | | | | 80 |
| 9 | 9 | | | | | | | | | |
| 10 | | | | | 50 | | | | | |

**1** 40 − 16 = _____

**2**
$$574 \atop +\,353$$       $$326 \atop +\,468$$

**3** Continue the pattern.

600  700  _____  _____

_____  _____  _____

**4** Write the correct symbols in the circles to complete the number sentence.

6 ◯ 4 ◯ 8 = 2

**5** There are 7 people in the Garcia family. Each of them ate 11 pretzels. How many pretzels did they eat in all?

_____ pretzels

Show your work.

**1** 9 × 5 = _____

_____ ÷ 9 = 5

**2**
$$286 \atop -\ \ 79$$     [   ]

[   ] $$+\ \ 79 \over 286$$

**3** Circle the digit in the ones place. Draw a line under the digit in the hundreds place.

694

**4** 8 cups = _____ quarts

◯ 1    ◯ 2    ◯ 3    ◯ 4

**5** One pencil costs 9¢. How much will Nick have to pay for eight pencils?

_____¢

If Nick pays with three quarters, how much change will he get back?

_____¢

**1**  4 x 8 = _____

8 x 4 = _____

**2**   385
+ 74

$-385$
$\phantom{-3}74$

**3**  What fraction is shaded?

□
8

**4**  Write the number for two hundred fifty-three.

_____

**5**  Gumdrops cost 8¢ for 2. How many gumdrops can Angel buy with 32¢?

_____ gumdrops

Show your work.

**1**  32 – 6 = _____

**2**  6 x _____ = 48        6)48

**3**  Color $\frac{1}{3}$ .

□ □ □ □ □ □

**4**  Write the correct symbol in the circle.

< = >

592 ◯ 586

1,036 ◯ 1,306

**5**  Eduardo had 72 jelly beans. He gave 8 jelly beans to each of his friends. How many friends were given jelly beans?

_____ friends

## ➤ Activity 1

Alicia has five dogs. She wants to give three bones to each of them.
How many bones will Alicia need?

**1.** Use pictures to solve the problem.

**2.** Use addition to solve the problem.

**3.** Use multiplication to solve the problem.

## ➤ Activity 2

Multiply by 2.

2 x 0 = _____     2 x 1 = _____     2 x 2 = _____

2 x 3 = _____     2 x 4 = _____     2 x 5 = _____

2 x 6 = _____     2 x 7 = _____     2 x 8 = _____

2 x 9 = _____     2 x 10 = _____    2 x 11 = _____

Will any number x2 always be an even number?      ○ **yes**      ○ **no**

1  75 + 22 = _____

   95 + 22 = _____

2
```
   384        1,000
 - 106       -  500
```

3   $\frac{1}{2}$ of 6 = _____

4  Round the numbers to the nearest hundred.

     189 is almost _____

     155 is almost _____

5  There are 24 dogs in the dog show. It is the first show for one-third of the dogs. How many dogs are in their first show?

     _____ dogs

1  9 x 6 = _____

   9 x 7 = _____

2
```
   86         186
  +47        +147
```

3  Circle the odd numbers.

   23   81   18   34   65

4  467¢ = $_____

5  Ellery and Kim have a lemonade stand. They charge 25¢ per cupful. Nine people each bought one cup of lemonade today. How much money did Ellery and Kim collect?

     $_____

**1** 104 – 14 = _____

**2** _____ × 4 = 36    4)36

**3** Find the perimeter.

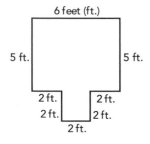

_____ feet

**4** 4 tens and 9 ones = _____

7 tens and 6 ones = _____

**5** Write number sentences using **7**, **3**, and **21**.

_____ × _____ = _____

_____ × _____ = _____

_____ ÷ _____ = _____

_____ ÷ _____ = _____

**1** _____ × 9 = 45

45 ÷ 9 = _____

**2**   32        30
        28        30
      +46       +50

**3** How many  ?   ○ 2
                                        ○ 3
                                        ○ 4

**4** Draw a different line of symmetry on each shape.

**5** It has been snowing for three days. It snowed six inches on Monday, five inches yesterday, and four inches today. About how much has it snowed altogether?

○ less than 1 foot

○ more than 1 foot

➤ **Activity 1**

| Shells We Collected | = 2 shells |
|---|---|
| **Mark** 🐚🐚🐚 | **Tonia** 🐚🐚🐚🐚🐚 |
| **Carlos** 🐚🐚🐚🐚 | **Mei Ling** 🐚🐚 |

1. How many shells does each symbol stand for? _____ shells

2. How many fewer shells did Mark find than Tonia? _____ shells

3. How many more shells did Mark and Carlos find together than Mei Ling? _____ shells

➤ **Activity 2**

Round to the nearest 100.

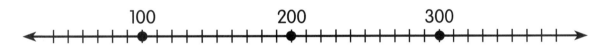

98 is almost _____    120 is almost _____

151 is almost _____    189 is almost _____

278 is almost _____    249 is almost _____

336 is almost _____    303 is almost _____

**1** 5 x 8 = _____

6 x 8 = _____

**2**
$$819 \\ -726$$          $$927 \\ -534$$

**3** Color $\frac{4}{5}$.

**4** 10 hundreds = _____

11 hundreds = _____

**5** Kaitlyn had 84 stickers. She gave 35 stickers to her best friend. How many stickers did she have left?

_____ stickers

Show your work.

---

**1** 3 x _____ = 24

24 ÷ 3 = _____

**2**
$$588 \\ +281$$          $$\square \\ -588 \\ \overline{281}$$

**3** 1,450 – _____ = 0

**4** How long is the pencil?

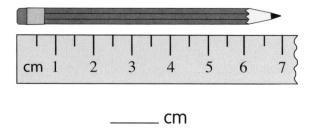

_____ cm

**5** Antonio eats 1 slice of pizza in 3 minutes. How long will it take Antonio to eat 4 slices?

_____ minutes

1. $550 - 241 =$ \_\_\_\_\_

2. $5 \times$ \_\_\_\_\_ $= 50$ $\quad 5\overline{)50}$

3. Color $\frac{1}{4}$.

$\frac{1}{4}$ of 8 = \_\_\_\_\_

4. What is the distance from **a** to **b** called?

a ●————————————————● b

○ line

○ angle

○ line segment

5. Maya made 36 rag dolls to sell. She sold half of the dolls. How many dolls does she have left?

\_\_\_\_\_ dolls

1. $6 \times 7 = 7 \times$ \_\_\_\_\_

2. $\quad \$3.55 \qquad \$4.22$
   $+ \ 1.29 \qquad - \ 2.13$

3. Divide the octagon into fourths. Color $\frac{3}{4}$.

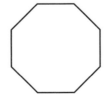

4. $684 -$ \_\_\_\_\_ $= 684$

5. In the morning, it takes Dad a half hour to dress, 15 minutes to eat breakfast, and 10 minutes to fix his lunch. If he gets up at 7:00 a.m., at what time will he be ready to leave for work? Show your answer on the clock.

## Ice-Cream Sundae

| | |
|---|---|
| ice cream ................. 60¢ per scoop | whipped cream ........................ 24¢ |
| banana ...................... 10¢ per slice | walnuts ................................. 18¢ |
| chocolate sauce ...................... 15¢ | cherry ................................... 20¢ |

**1.** Read the sign. How much does this sundae cost?

2 scoops ice cream = _____

2 banana slices　　= _____

chocolate sauce　　= _____

whipped cream　　= _____

Cost $_____

**2.** Make your own. How much does your sundae cost?

| My Sundae | My ingredients: | Cost: each item |
|---|---|---|
| | _____ | _____ |
| | _____ | _____ |
| | _____ | _____ |
| | _____ | _____ |
| | _____ | _____ |
| | _____ | _____ |

Cost $_____

**1** $9 \times \underline{\quad} = 18$

$18 \div 9 = \underline{\quad}$

**2**
$$\begin{array}{r} 845 \\ -\ 36 \\ \hline \boxed{\phantom{000}} \end{array}$$

$$\begin{array}{r} \boxed{\phantom{000}} \\ +\ 36 \\ \hline 845 \end{array}$$

**3** Circle the best estimate.

$$196 - 54 = ?$$

○ 100    ○ 150    ○ 200

**4** Count by thousands.

1,000  2,000  _____  _____

_____  _____  _____

**5** Andrew had 24¢. Then his mom gave him a quarter and his dad gave him 43¢. How much money does he have now?

\_\_\_\_\_¢

**1** $8 \times 9 = \underline{\quad}$

$\underline{\quad} \div 8 = 9$

**2** $9{,}463 + 1{,}025 = \underline{\quad\quad}$

**3** Write a word problem for **3 x 4 = 12**.

_____

_____

_____

_____

**4** Expand the numbers.

$683 = \underline{\quad} + \underline{\quad} + \underline{\quad}$

$809 = \underline{\quad} + \underline{\quad}$

**5** Terri has three kinds of cats. The Siamese weighs 4.5 kilograms (kg), the tabby weighs 3.6 kilograms, and the Persian weighs 2.3 kilograms. How much do the cats weigh altogether?

\_\_\_\_\_ kg

**1**  1,005 + 2,025 = _____

**2**
```
  654        893
– 364      – 422
```

**3**  What is the name of this solid figure?

○ cone

○ sphere

○ cylinder

**4**  Write an even number that is greater than 10 and less than 20.

_____

**5**  One box of popcorn costs $0.65. How much will three boxes cost?

$_____

Show your work.

**1**  9 x 8 = _____

9 x 9 = _____

**2**  4 x _____ = 32      4)‾32‾

**3**

= $_____

**4**

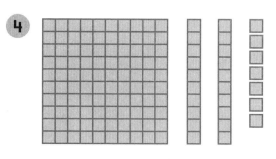

= _____

**5**  Whale shark eggs are about 30 cm long. Ostrich eggs are about 18 cm long. About how much longer is a whale shark egg than an ostrich egg?

_____ cm

Use the graph to answer the questions.

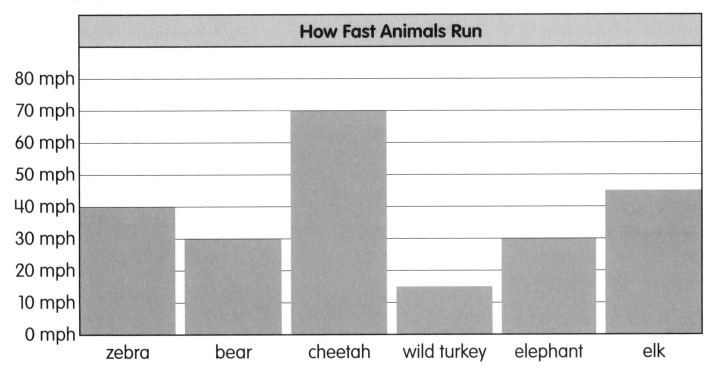

1. Which animal is the fastest?

   ○ zebra

   ○ cheetah

   ○ elk

2. Which animals run twice as fast as a wild turkey?

   ○ zebra and bear

   ○ bear and elephant

   ○ elephant and elk

3. How much faster can a cheetah run than an elephant? _____ mph

4. How much slower is a wild turkey than a zebra? _____ mph

**1**   $9 \times \underline{\hspace{1cm}} = 81$

    $81 \div 9 = \underline{\hspace{1cm}}$

**2**
$$\begin{array}{r} 46 \\ 13 \\ +\,50 \\ \hline \end{array} \qquad \begin{array}{r} 50 \\ 10 \\ +\,50 \\ \hline \end{array}$$

**3**   What fraction is shaded?

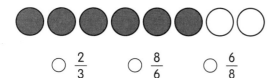

    ○ $\frac{2}{3}$     ○ $\frac{8}{6}$     ○ $\frac{6}{8}$

**4**   $(8 + 6) + 5 = \underline{\hspace{1cm}}$

    $8 + (6 + 5) = \underline{\hspace{1cm}}$

**5**   Gianna collected 24 pounds of glass bottles. A recycling plant paid her 4¢ for each pound. How much money was Gianna paid for all the bottles she collected?

        $\underline{\hspace{2cm}}$ ¢

---

**1**   $3 \times 7 = \underline{\hspace{1cm}}$

    $4 \times 7 = \underline{\hspace{1cm}}$

**2**
$$\begin{array}{r} 460 \\ -\ \ 92 \\ \hline \end{array} \qquad \begin{array}{r} 521 \\ -\ \ 82 \\ \hline \end{array}$$

**3**   Write the correct symbol in the circle.

    <    =    >

    1,264 ◯ 1,642

**4**

        = $ \underline{\hspace{2cm}}

**5**   It is Alondra's birthday. She got $15.75 from her grandparents, $13.00 from her aunt, and $11.25 from her uncle. How much money did she receive altogether?

        $ \underline{\hspace{2cm}}

1. 700 − 450 = _____

   1,200 − 300 = _____

2. 
   $$1,234 + 4,827$$
   
   $$3,821 + 2,134$$

3. Marta can pick 10 baskets of peaches in one hour. How long will it take her to pick 60 baskets of peaches?

   _____ hours

4. Draw an **X** on the digit in the hundreds place. Draw a line under the digit in the thousands place. Circle the digit in the ones place.

   6,483

5. Circle the best unit for measuring the height of a 10-story building.

   ○ inches          ○ centimeters

   ○ feet            ○ pounds

---

1. 7 x 8 = _____

   8 x 7 = _____

2. 8 x _____ = 72          8⟌72

3. Circle the names for the shaded parts.

   $\frac{1}{2}$     $\frac{1}{3}$     $\frac{2}{3}$     $\frac{3}{6}$

4. Circle the number six hundred sixty-two.

   662     60,062     6,062

5. The Moore family spent $23.52 to buy lunch. The Miller family spent $24.62. How much did both families spend altogether?

   $_____

➤ **Activity 1**

A factory makes bicycles every day. The colors of the bicycles are black, red, blue, green, and purple. Red bikes are the favorite of most children. How many days would it take the factory to make 500 bicycles?

Which sentence is needed to answer the question?

○ More boys than girls ride bikes.

○ The factory is open 10 hours a day.

○ The factory can make 100 bikes each day.

Now answer the question.

_____ days

➤ **Activity 2**

Mr. Lau works at the bicycle factory. He gets a half-hour lunch break. If he goes to lunch at 12:32, at what time does he need to be back?

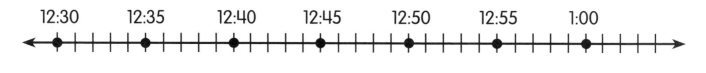

Answer:

**1**  $7 \times \underline{\hspace{1cm}} = 63$

$63 \div 7 = \underline{\hspace{1cm}}$

**2**
```
   536        604
 - 274      - 253
```

**3**

$= \underline{\hspace{1cm}}$

**4**  Circle the even numbers.

16    21    44    38    57

**5**  A boa is 3 meters long. A python is 197 centimeters long.

Which snake is longer?

○ boa        ○ python

How much longer?    $\underline{\hspace{1cm}}$ cm

**1**  $10 \times 5 = \underline{\hspace{1cm}}$

$10 \times 6 = \underline{\hspace{1cm}}$

**2**
```
   555        727
 + 168      + 209
```

**3**  Twenty soldiers are marching in a line. In what place is soldier number 12?

○ second   ○ twentieth   ○ twelfth

**4**  The decimal point is missing in the amount below. Mark the answer that shows dollars and cents.

$1260

○ $1.260      ○ $126.0      ○ $12.60

**5**  Lisa made 240 popcorn balls. She put 8 popcorn balls in each box. How many boxes did Lisa use?

$\underline{\hspace{1cm}}$ boxes

**1** 6 x 6 = _____

7 x 7 = _____

**2**
```
  245        360
  520        201
+ 315      + 429
```

**3** Spend $2.75     Pay with $5.00

Get back $_____

**4** Continue the pattern.

1,250  1,300  1,350  _____

_____  _____

**5** School starts at 8:55 a.m. Connor leaves home at 8:15 a.m. It takes him 35 minutes to get to school. Will he be on time?

○ **yes**     ○ **no**

---

**1** 65 – 15 – 20 = _____

**2** 6)42     6)48     6)54

**3** Write the correct symbol in the circle.

< = >

35 + 15 ◯ 75 – 40

**4** What time will it be 20 minutes later?

   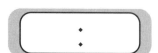

**5** Jason has a savings account at the bank. Every week he takes half of his $4.00 allowance to the bank. How much will he save in ten weeks?

$_____

➤ **Activity 1**

1. Hot dogs come in packages of 10.
   Complete the function table.

| Number of Packages | 1 | 2 | 3 | 4 | 5 | 6 | 7 | 8 |
|---|---|---|---|---|---|---|---|---|
| Number of Hot Dogs | 10 | 20 | | | | | | |

2. Circle the operations you can use.

   addition      subtraction      multiplication      division

➤ **Activity 2**

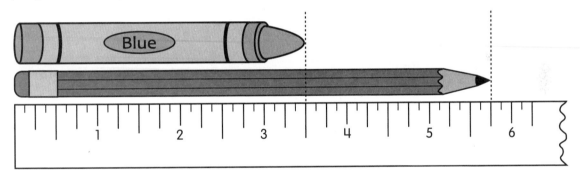

1. The pencil is _____ inches long.

2. The crayon is _____ inches long.

3. The pencil is _____ inches longer than the crayon.

4. Estimate the length of the eraser.

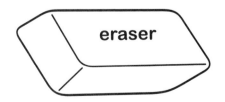

   ○ 1 inch
   ○ 2 inches
   ○ 3 inches

**1**  $4 \times 2 \times 6 =$ _____

**2**
```
  328        487
－ 69      － 98
```

**3**  Which shape has 8 sides of equal length?

    ○ pentagon     ○ octagon

Draw the shape.

**4**  Continue the pattern.

14, 21, 28, _____ _____ _____

_____ _____

**5**  I am an even number between 10 and 19. I am less than 16 and more than 13. What number am I?

_____

**1**  $30 \div 6 =$ _____

**2**
```
  300        200
  200        700
＋500      ＋400
```

**3**  Does the house have symmetry?

    ○ **yes**     ○ **no**

**4**  Round the numbers to the nearest hundred.

193 is almost _____

230 is almost _____

**5**  The diameter of the planet Venus is about 650 km smaller than the diameter of Earth. If Earth's diameter is about 13,000 km, what is the diameter of Venus?

about _____ km

**1** 9 × _____ = 54

54 ÷ 9 = _____

**2**   $4.65        $9.22
   − 3.79       − 5.83

**3** Which clock shows quarter to 12?

◯            ◯            ◯

**4** 927 = _____ hundreds

_____ tens

_____ ones

**5** Evan can do one sit-up every 5 seconds. How long will it take him to do 24 sit-ups?

_____ minutes

Show your work.

---

**1** 12 × 2 = _____

12 × 3 = _____

**2**   2,086        3,328
   + 1,529      + 2,709

**3** Draw two shapes that are congruent.

**4** Write the correct symbol in the circle.

16 ounces ◯ 1 pound

5 inches ◯ 5 centimeters

**5** Rama and her friends each ate 7 cherries. A total of 28 cherries were eaten. How many children ate the cherries?

_____ children

## ➤ Activity 1

Complete the table.
How many treats will each person get?

☺ = 1 person

| | | |
|---|---|---|
| There are 25 pretzels. | ☺ ☺ ☺ ☺ ☺ | _____ pretzels each |
| There are 24 jelly beans. | ☺ ☺ ☺ ☺ | _____ jelly beans each |
| There are 18 cookies. | ☺ ☺ ☺ | _____ cookies each |
| There are 16 peanuts. | ☺ ☺ | _____ peanuts each |

## ➤ Activity 2

Which number line shows $\frac{1}{4}$?

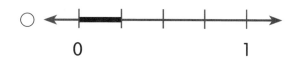

Which number line shows $\frac{2}{3}$?

**1**  256 + 437 = _____

**2**
```
   30
 x  3        3)30
```

**3**  Color $\frac{1}{4}$ of the figure.

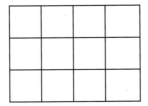

**4**  Continue the pattern.

3  5  8  10  _____  _____  _____

**5**  Corey, Terry, and Mia each have 6 pieces of gum. How much gum do they have altogether? Mark the **two** ways that you can find the answer.

○ add          ○ subtract

○ divide       ○ multiply

**1**  $5.54 – $2.75 = $_____

**2**  2 x _____ = 40        2)40

**3**  Tomás bought 4 packages of pencils. There were 12 pencils in each package. How many pencils did Tomás buy?

_____ pencils

**4**  46 + _____ = 60

**5**  What is the perimeter?

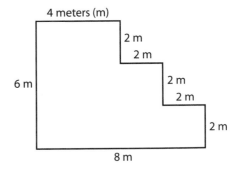

_____ meters

**1**  364 – 192 = _____

**2**  $\begin{array}{r} 1,462 \\ 3,017 \\ + 5,236 \\ \hline \end{array}$

**3**  Draw an **X** on three shapes that have four corners and four sides.

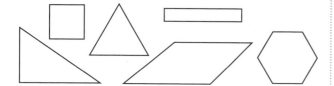

**4**  (2 × 2) × 3 = _____

   2 × (2 × 3) = _____

**5**  Five hundred ninety people came to the aquarium on Saturday. Three hundred eighty people came on Sunday. Estimate how many people came to the aquarium during the weekend.

   ○  about 900 people

   ○  about 500 people

   ○  about 1,000 people

**1**  7 × _____ = 28

   28 ÷ 7 = _____

**2**  $\begin{array}{r} 14 \\ \times\ 2 \\ \hline \end{array}$       $\begin{array}{r} 15 \\ \times\ 2 \\ \hline \end{array}$

**3**  4 × 0 = _____       9 × 0 = _____

   52 × 0 = _____       136 × 0 = _____

   Any number multiplied by 0 = _____.

**4**  Write the correct symbol in the circle.

   < = >

   9,050 ◯ 5,090

   1,000 ◯ 500 + 500

**5**  Write a word problem for **15 – 10 = 5**.

   _____

   _____

   _____

➤ **Activity 1**

At the fruit stand, strawberries come in three sizes. A small basket holds 15 strawberries. A middle-sized basket holds 30 strawberries. The largest basket holds 45 strawberries. Jacob bought three baskets.

1. What is the smallest number of strawberries
   Jacob could have?               _____ strawberries

2. What is the largest number of strawberries
   Jacob could have?               _____ strawberries

➤ **Activity 2**

Find the area.

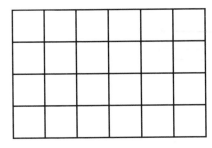

- ○ 30 square units
- ○ 20 square units
- ○ 24 square units

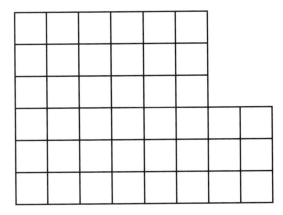

- ○ 50 square units
- ○ 42 square units
- ○ 36 square units

Daily Math Practice

1. $6.50 + $6.50 = $_____

   $7.75 + $7.75 = $_____

2. 
   ```
     325
   -  68
   _____
   ```
   ```
       _____
   +   68
   _____
       325
   ```

3. 325 x 1 = _____     1,000 x 1 = _____

   Any number multiplied by 1 equals itself.

   ○ yes     ○ no

4. Write the correct symbol in the circle.

   < = >

   9 x 3 ◯ 9 ÷ 3

   3 x 5 ◯ 15 ÷ 3

5. Julian raises rabbits. He has 8 does, and each doe has 6 babies. How many baby rabbits does Julian have altogether?

   _____ baby rabbits

Daily Math Practice

1. 11 x 6 = _____

   11 x 7 = _____

2. 
   ```
     9,087          8,246
   - 3,647        - 6,048
   ```

3. Write four ways to make **20**.

   _____ x _____          _____ x _____

   _____ x _____          _____ x _____

4. Circle the best estimate for the answer to **212 + 486**.

   600     700     800

5. Kira has 9 bags of shells. Each bag holds 9 shells. How many shells does Kira have in all?

   _____ shells

Daily Math Practice • EMC 752 • © Evan-Moor Corp.

1  $6 \times$ _____ $= 48$

  $48 \div 6 =$ _____

2
$\begin{array}{r} \$4.75 \\ - \ 2.25 \\ \hline \end{array}$
$\begin{array}{r} \$5.50 \\ - \ 2.50 \\ \hline \end{array}$

3  Circle six hundred ninety-seven.

  60,097    697    6,097

4  Write the correct symbol in the circle.

  < = >

  $5.00 ◯ 8 quarters

  $1.50 ◯ 30 nickels

5  How many erasers can Zoey buy if each one costs 25 cents, and she has 2 quarters, 3 dimes, and a penny?

  _____ erasers

1  $5,066 + 1,749 =$ _____

2  $7 \times$ _____ $= 35$      $7\overline{)35}$

3  Continue the pattern.

  1,000  1,100  1,200  _____

  _____  _____  _____

4  Write **x** or $\div$ in the circle.

  $54 ◯ 9 = 6$

5  There were 48 children at the picnic. They formed six teams of equal size to play games. How many children were on each team?

  _____ children

  Show your work.

➤ **Activity 1**

Aunt Emily planted 6 rows of 9 daisies and 8 rows of 7 tulips
in her garden this year. Last year she planted 100 flowers.
Did she plant more or less flowers this year?

        ○ more     ○ less

How many more or less?    _____ flowers

➤ **Activity 2**

A quadrilateral is a plane shape with four sides and four angles.
Color all the shapes that are quadrilaterals.

**1**   10 x 7 = _____

   10 x 8 = _____

**2**   836        909
    +475       +119

**3**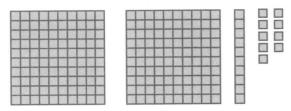

   = _____

**4** Continue the pattern.

   150  175  200  _____  _____  _____

**5** There are 24 students in Tanisha's class. She wants to give one cookie to each student. If there are 8 cookies in a package, how many packages will Tanisha need to buy?

   _____ packages

**1**   _____ x 6 = 36

   36 ÷ 6 = _____

**2**   224
    163
   +  32

**3**   1 thousand + 6 hundreds + 3 tens

   + 4 ones = _____

**4** Write ten dollars and six cents with the decimal point in the correct place.

   _____

**5** A fisherman caught 24 fish. He divided the fish equally among 6 friends. How many fish did he give to each friend?

   _____ fish

   Show your work.

**1**   7 x _____ = 49      7)49

**2**   4,674      6,297
    − 2,493     − 1,503

**3**   Circle the fractions that equal **1**.

$\frac{2}{2}$    $\frac{5}{6}$    $\frac{8}{8}$    $\frac{4}{4}$    $\frac{3}{6}$

**4**   Write the time shown on the clock two different ways.

_____ minutes after _____

_____ minutes before _____

**5**   Write the number that is two more than 7 times 6.

_____

**1**   21 x 3 = _____

21 ÷ 3 = _____

**2**   455      626
   − 170     − 107

**3**   Mrs. Chan hired 4 boys to paint her fence. She paid each boy $12.00. How much did it cost Mrs. Chan to have the fence painted?

$_____

**4**   Write the number in expanded form.

471 = _____ + _____ + _____

**5**   Find the area of the rectangle.

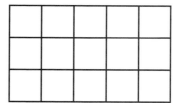

_____ square units

## ➤ Activity 1

Look at the coins. Multiply each coin by the number next to it.
Write the total value on the line.

5 x ⬤ = $_____        3 x ⬤ = $_____        12 x ⬤ = $_____

19 x ⬤ = $_____        12 x ⬤ = $_____

## ➤ Activity 2

How many products can you write in one minute?

| 10 | 11 | 12 | 15 | 19 | 20 | 31 |
|----|----|----|----|----|----|----|
| x 2 | x 3 | x 4 | x 2 | x 1 | x 3 | x 0 |

$11 \times 6 =$ _____        $27 \times 2 =$ _____        $4 \times 12 =$ _____        $9 \times 10 =$ _____

| 25 | 63 | 41 | 37 | 55 | 10 | 14 |
|----|----|----|----|----|----|----|
| x 2 | x 3 | x 4 | x 5 | x 2 | x 8 | x 3 |

_____ correct

**1** 10 x 8 = _____

_____ ÷ 10 = 8

**2**
```
  6,307        7,229
+   984      +   806
```

**3** Color $\frac{2}{5}$ .

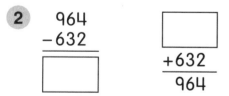

**4** Had:

Spent: $1.75

Had left: $_____

**5** Juan's team had batting practice today. Each player got to swing at 7 pitches. If 9 players were at practice, how many balls were pitched?

_____ balls

**1** 9 x _____ = 72

72 ÷ 9 = _____

**2**
```
  964            ☐
-632         +632
 ☐           964
```

**3** 7 thousands, 8 hundreds, and 5 ones

= _____

**4** $\frac{7}{10}$ = ?

○ 0.7

○ 0.07

○ 1.07

**5** One cup of popcorn kernels makes four cups of popped corn. There are eight cups of kernels in a bag. How many cups of popped corn will one bag of kernels make?

_____ cups

**1** 5,265 − 1,638 = _____

**2** 8 × _____ = 64　　　8)64‾

**3** Write the time that is 5 minutes later.

4:20 _____　　　6:15 _____

9:25 _____　　　2:40 _____

3:46 _____　　　12:01 _____

**4** Circle the largest number.

10,560　　　10,422　　　10,920

**5** The ballgame started at 10:00 a.m. and ended at 1:30 p.m. How long did the ballgame last?

○ 1 hour

○ $2\frac{1}{2}$ hours

○ $3\frac{1}{2}$ hours

**1** twenty + thirty + ten = ?

○ forty　　　○ fifty　　　○ sixty

**2**
```
  32        51
x  4       x 2
```

**3** It takes 15 minutes to bake 1 dozen cookies. How long will it take to bake 3 dozen cookies?

_____ minutes

**4** If 45 ÷ 9 = 5, then 45 ÷ 5 = _____.

**5** Are these shapes congruent?

 　　○ **yes**　　○ **no**

Explain your answer.

_____

_____

_____

_____

Tara collected information about her classmates' birthdays.
Use the information to complete the bar graph.

| Class Birthdays | |
|---|---|
| January II | July I |
| February IIII | August III |
| March I | September II |
| April II | October III |
| May | November |
| June 卌 | December III |

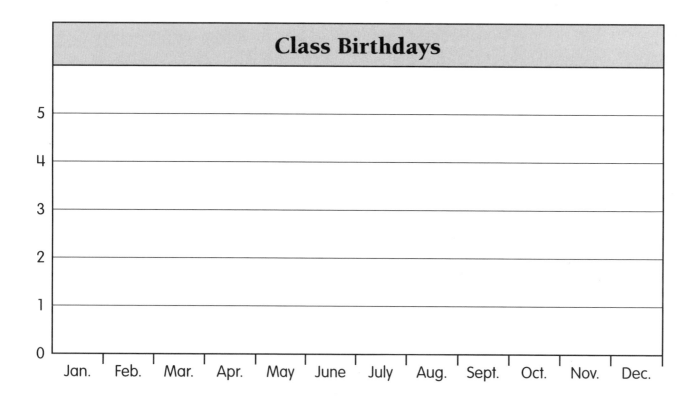

1. 6,805 + 2,300 = _____

2. $\begin{array}{r} 32 \\ \times\ 3 \\ \hline \end{array}$    $\begin{array}{r} 24 \\ \times\ 2 \\ \hline \end{array}$

3. For each number, circle the digit in the thousands place. Underline the digit in the tens place.

   5,629        12,463

4. There are _____ centimeters in a meter.

5. Use only **3**, **4**, and **5** to complete the number sentences.

   _____ × _____ − _____ = 11

   _____ × _____ + _____ = 17

   _____ × _____ × _____ = 60

   _____ + (_____ × _____) = 19

1. 40 ÷ 5 = _____

   40 ÷ 8 = _____

2. $\begin{array}{r} 403 \\ -268 \\ \hline \end{array}$    The answer is greater than 200.

   ○ **yes**        ○ **no**

3. Write the number for twelve dollars and sixty-eight cents.

   $_____

4. (6 × 2) × 1 = _____

   6 × (2 × 1) = _____

5. A ticket to the basketball game costs $8.25. How much will three tickets cost?

   $_____

   Show your work.

1  $7 \times \underline{\quad} = 56$    $7\overline{)56}$

2  fifty – twenty = ?
   ○ thirty
   ○ thirteen
   ○ twenty-five

3  Write the fractions in order from smallest to largest.

   $\frac{1}{2}$    $\frac{1}{6}$    $\frac{1}{3}$    $\frac{1}{4}$

   \_\_\_\_\_ \_\_\_\_\_ \_\_\_\_\_ \_\_\_\_\_

4  Write **x** or ÷ in the circle.

   $81 \bigcirc 9 = 9$

5  How many pears?

   2 dozen = \_\_\_\_\_

   $2\frac{1}{2}$ dozen = \_\_\_\_\_

1  $20 \times 4 = \underline{\quad}$

2  $\begin{array}{r} \frac{7}{8} \\ -\frac{4}{8} \\ \hline \end{array}$    $\begin{array}{r} \frac{11}{12} \\ -\frac{10}{12} \\ \hline \end{array}$

3  Write the number that is one more.

   7,804 _____    3,069 _____

   5,590 _____    1,999 _____

4  $\frac{1}{4}$ of 12 = \_\_\_\_\_

5  Erika's class went to the zoo. They saw 54 different animals. Half of the animals came from Africa. How many animals were from Africa?

   \_\_\_\_\_ animals

   Show your work.

➤ **Activity 1**

Look at each set. Are the shaded parts equal? Circle **yes** or **no**.

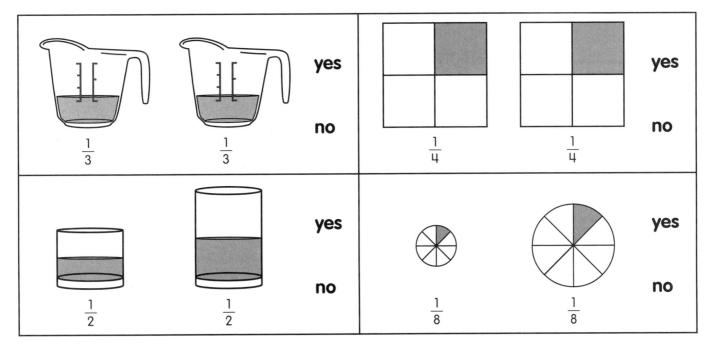

➤ **Activity 2**

1. Students at Lakewood School want to play four-square. Show how they can paint 2 lines in the box to make fourths.

2. Now draw 2 more lines to show a way to make eighths.

**1**

$\frac{4}{6}$      $\frac{4}{9}$

$+ \frac{1}{6}$     $+ \frac{2}{9}$

**2** $9\overline{)63}$      $9 \times \underline{\hspace{1cm}} = 63$

**3** Which decimal equals $\frac{6}{10}$?

○ 6.0    ○ 0.6    ○ 10.6

**4** Which number is nine thousand forty?

○ 940      ○ 9,004

○ 9,040      ○ 9,400

**5** Dad wants to build a fence around our garden. The garden has 4 sides that are each 8 meters long. What is the perimeter of the garden?

\_\_\_\_\_ meters

**1** $13 \times 4 = \underline{\hspace{1cm}}$

$20 \times 6 = \underline{\hspace{1cm}}$

**2**

   334      421

−  95     −  87

**3** If $27 \div 9 = 3$, then $9 \times 3 = \underline{\hspace{1cm}}$.

**4** What fraction is shaded?

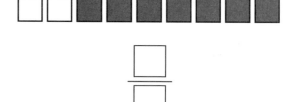

$$\frac{\square}{\square}$$

**5** A gray whale dove 129 feet on its first dive, 360 feet on its second dive, and 277 feet on its third dive. How many feet did the whale dive in all?

_____ feet

**1**  $24 \div 8 =$ _____

   $32 \div 8 =$ _____

**2**    609          709
      $-345$        $-345$

**3**  How many thousands are in 24,692?

      _____ thousands

**4**  Count by nines.

   9 _____  _____  _____  _____

   _____  _____  _____  _____  _____

**5**  A farmer brought 15 watermelons to a picnic. Each watermelon was cut into 6 slices. If each person ate only one slice, how many people had watermelon?

      _____ people

**1**  $7 \times 9 =$ _____

   _____ $\div 7 = 9$

**2**    373
      $+479$
      [   ]

      $-373$
      479

**3**  Draw an **X** on the symmetrical shape.

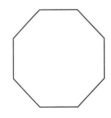
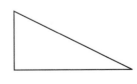

**4**  Continue the pattern.

   1 5 2 6 _____  _____  _____

**5**  Will and Hailey are building a doghouse for Buddy. They went to the lumberyard and spent $22.42 for wood. If they gave the clerk $25.00, how much change did they receive?

      $_____

**1.** Circle the right angle.

**2.** Circle the angle that is greater than a right angle.

**3.** Circle the angle that is less than a right angle.

**4.** Look at each circled angle. Mark the answer that describes it.

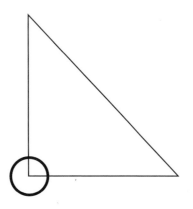

     ○ a right angle

     ○ greater than a right angle

     ○ less than a right angle

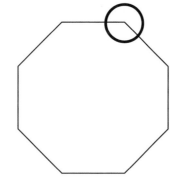

     ○ a right angle

     ○ greater than a right angle

     ○ less than a right angle

1. 81 − 66 = _____

2. 
```
   465        1,329
  +887       +  708
```

3. Write the fraction for the shaded parts **two** ways.

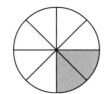

□/□ = □/□

4. Write the number in expanded form.

2,086

_____

5. A sea otter ate a total of 35 sea stars in 5 days. If she ate the same number of sea stars each day, how many did she eat in one day?

_____ sea stars

1. 42 × 2 = _____

2. 
$$2\frac{1}{3} \qquad 3\frac{1}{8}$$
$$+2\frac{1}{3} \qquad +3\frac{3}{8}$$

3. Round the numbers to the nearest 10.

93 is almost _____

38 is almost _____

4. Number the lengths in order from shortest to longest.

2 ft.    1 yd.    9 ft.    18 in.    2 yd.

_____ _____ _____ _____ _____

5. If there are 365 days in one year, how many days are there in three years?

_____ days

Show your work.

1    24 + 12 + 16 = _____

2    28          33
     x  3        x  4

3    Mark the ray.

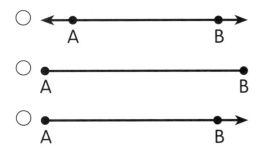

4    Write sixteen dollars and eighty-four cents in the number form.

     $_____

5    Brayden earned $10.00 mowing lawns. He bought a birthday present for his sister that cost $5.50. How much money does Brayden have left?

     $_____

---

1    3)‾10‾          5)‾26‾

2    2,568          4,092
   + 1,425        + 1,337

3    Which number is ninety-four thousand five hundred?

     ○ 90,450        ○  9,450

     ○ 95,400        ○ 94,500

4    How many inches are there in 5 feet?

     _____ inches

5    The regular price of a kite is $9.60. Today it is on sale at $\frac{1}{3}$ off the regular price. What is the sale price of the kite?

     $_____

➤ **Activity 1**

Write the equivalent fraction and decimal for each amount.

| Amount | Fraction | Decimal |
|---|---|---|
| 4 cents | $\frac{4}{100}$ | $0.04 |
| 12 cents | | |
| 25 cents | | |
| 50 cents | | |
| 100 cents | | |

➤ **Activity 2**

**1.** How many quotients can you write in one minute?

$5\overline{)25}$ $\qquad$ $9\overline{)18}$ $\qquad$ $3\overline{)21}$ $\qquad$ $4\overline{)32}$ $\qquad$ $9\overline{)81}$

$60 \div 6 = \underline{\quad}$ $\qquad$ $40 \div 5 = \underline{\quad}$ $\qquad$ $90 \div 10 = \underline{\quad}$

**2.** Solve with remainders.

$5\overline{)11}$ $\qquad$ $6\overline{)43}$ $\qquad$ $5\overline{)51}$ $\qquad$ $8\overline{)66}$ $\qquad$ $7\overline{)55}$

$\underline{\quad}$ correct

**1** 370 − 190 = \_\_\_\_\_

**2**    $3\frac{6}{12}$      $2\frac{1}{2}$

   $+\,7\frac{4}{12}$    $+\,3\frac{1}{2}$

**3** Color boxes to show the fraction $\frac{8}{12}$.

**4** How many quarts are in $4\frac{1}{2}$ gallons?

\_\_\_\_\_ quarts

**5** Shannon's birthday is on May 10. Paolo's birthday is two weeks later. What is the date of Paolo's birthday?

_____

Show your work.

---

**1** 29 ÷ 7 = \_\_\_\_\_

   31 ÷ 10 = \_\_\_\_\_

**2**    662      728

   − 275    − 499

**3** Circle the shapes that are congruent.

**4** Mark the number word for **163**.

   ○ one hundred three

   ○ one hundred thirty

   ○ one hundred sixty-three

**5** A store sells worms for fishing. A box of 50 worms costs $2.95. Mr. Reyes bought 8 boxes. How many worms did he get?

\_\_\_\_\_ worms

**1**  6)‾55        7)‾36        9)‾73

**2**    426          515
       x   3        x   2

**3**  Circle the shape that has symmetry.

**4**  Write the number three thousand nine hundred thirty-four.

_____

**5**  Dr. Light performed an operation that started at 2:30 p.m. and lasted 2 hours and 20 minutes. At what time was the operation over?

○ 4:30 p.m.

○ 4:45 p.m.

○ 4:50 p.m.

---

**1**  9 x 8 = _____

   74 ÷ 9 = _____

**2**   2,317        3,555
      + 1,925      + 1,255

**3**  Write the correct symbol in the circle.

   < = >

   16,439 ( ) 18,006

   20,001 ( ) 19,009

**4**  Write the number 352 in expanded form.

_____

**5**  I have:

Can I buy a game that costs $17.50?

○ **yes**        ○ **no**

➤ **Activity 1**

Sara is making individual fruit salads for the 6 people in her family. Each salad will have 3 apple slices, 6 banana chunks, 2 orange wedges, and 5 grapes. How many pieces of fruit will Sara prepare for all of the salads?

_____ pieces of fruit

Show your work.

➤ **Activity 2**

Two of the numbers below have a sum of 10 and a product of 24.

2    3    4    5    6

What are the numbers?    _____ and _____

Show your work.

1. 649 + 138 = _____

2.
   72        67
   x 4       x 5

3. Color the rhombus.

4.

   = _____ marshmallows

5. The ballgame lasted 3 hours and 16 minutes. It began at 1:30 p.m. At what time did it end?

   ○ 4:06 p.m.

   ○ 4:16 p.m.

   ○ 4:46 p.m.

1. 28 ÷ 5 = _____

   35 ÷ 3 = _____

2.
   643       726
   − 475     − 139

3. Circle 0.5 of the stars.

4. 200 + 90 + 8 = _____

5. A knot is a measure of speed used by ships. One knot equals 6,076.1 feet per hour. If a whale is swimming at 2 knots, how many feet will it travel in 1 hour?

   _____ feet

   Show your work.

1. $34 \times 3 =$ _____

   _____ $\div 3 = 34$

2.
$$\begin{array}{r} 4,736 \\ -\,3,510 \\ \hline \end{array}$$

$$\begin{array}{r} \phantom{0} \\ +\,3,510 \\ \hline 4,736 \end{array}$$

3. Find the area.

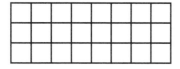

   _____ square units

4. $(5 \times 2) \times 6 =$ _____

   $5 \times (2 \times 6) =$ _____

5. On Sunday, 13 boats were in a race. There were 8 boats with 3 sailors each, 4 boats with 2 sailors each, and one boat with 5 sailors. What was the total number of sailors in the race?

   _____ sailors

   Show your work.

1. $7\overline{)44}$    $8\overline{)34}$

2.
$$\begin{array}{r} 8,336 \\ +\,1,937 \\ \hline \end{array} \qquad \begin{array}{r} 9,321 \\ +\,1,819 \\ \hline \end{array}$$

3. Write the correct symbol in the circle.

   < = >

   $\dfrac{1}{2} \bigcirc \dfrac{3}{6}$

4. Circle the spinner that has an equal chance of landing on black or white.

5. Divide the sum of the numbers on the fourth, second, and sixth apples by three.

   What is the quotient? _____

Mr. White asked each of his 24 students how they get to school. He collected these answers:

> walk – 12      ride bike – 3
>
> ride bus – 6     ride in a car – 3

**1.** Simplify each fraction in the table below. The first one has been done for you.

| walk | ride bike |
|---|---|
| $\dfrac{12}{24} = \dfrac{4}{8}$ | $\dfrac{3}{24} = \dfrac{\Box}{8}$ |
| **ride bus** | **ride in a car** |
| $\dfrac{6}{24} = \dfrac{\Box}{8}$ | $\dfrac{3}{24} = \dfrac{\Box}{8}$ |

**2.** Color the circle graph to show the simplified fraction for each way to get to school.

**walk** – red

**bus** – yellow

**bike** – blue

**car** – green

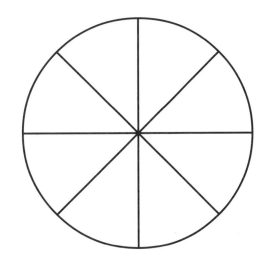

1. $24 \times 5 =$ _____

   _____ $\div 5 = 24$

2. 
   $386$
   $+292$
   
   $3,860$
   $+2,920$

3. Riley has 6 coins. Half of her coins are quarters, $\frac{1}{3}$ are nickels, and $\frac{1}{6}$ are dimes. How much money does Riley have?

   $ _____

4. Write four number sentences using **8**, **9**, and **72**.

   _____

   _____

   _____

   _____

5. Write the number seven hundred twenty-nine.

   _____

1. $65 \div 5 =$ _____

   $5 \times$ _____ $= 65$

2. 
   $3,980$
   $+2,356$
   
   $4,721$
   $+3,280$

3. 2 thousands, 5 hundreds, 6 ones

   $=$ _____

4. It is 6:00 p.m. What time will it be in 8 hours?

   ○ 8:00 a.m.

   ○ 2:00 a.m.

   ○ 2:00 p.m.

5. Model cars that cost $2.95 are on sale for $1.80. How much will David save if he buys two cars on sale?

   $ _____

**1** 9)59    8)63

**4** (9 x 7) x 2 = _____

9 x (7 x 2) = _____

**2**
```
  826
 -469
 ┌─────┐
 │     │
 └─────┘
```

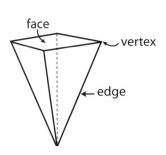
```
  469
+┌─────┐
 │     │
 └─────┘
  826
```

**5** It is 3 hours earlier in Oregon than in Maine. If it is 2:30 p.m. in Maine, what time is it in Oregon?

○ 11:30 a.m.

○ 11:30 p.m.

○ 11:00 a.m.

**3** How many?

_____ vertices

_____ edges

_____ faces

face

vertex

edge

**1** 8)49    9)57

**4** Circle the polygon that does **not** have a right angle.

**2**
```
  4,146
+ 3,289
```
```
  7,329
+ 1,216
```

**5** An explorer discovered a treasure chest. It contained 150 bags of silver coins. The explorer got to keep one-third of the bags of coins. How many bags did he get to keep?

_____ bags

**3** Draw an **X** on the digit in the tens place. Circle the digit in the thousands place.

9,782

Look at the figures to answer the questions.

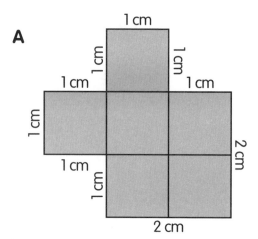

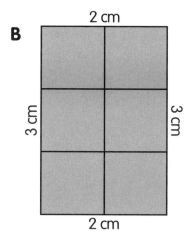

1. What is the area?

   **A** = _____ square cm

   **B** = _____ square cm

2. What is the perimeter?

   **A** = _____ cm

   **B** = _____ cm

3. Are the areas of figures **A** and **B** the same?

   ○ **yes**     ○ **no**

4. Are the perimeters of figures **A** and **B** the same?

   ○ **yes**     ○ **no**

1. $3\overline{)72}$     $2\overline{)81}$

2. 
$$\begin{array}{r} 3,148 \\ +4,907 \\ \hline \end{array}$$
$$\begin{array}{r} \boxed{\phantom{0000}} \\ -3,148 \\ \hline 4,907 \end{array}$$

3. How much of the group is shaded?

 $= \dfrac{\boxed{\phantom{0}}}{\boxed{\phantom{0}}}$

Write the fraction as a decimal.

_____

4. I am a shape with six faces and eight vertices. I can stack and slide. Which shape am I?

   ○ square

   ○ cube

   ○ pyramid

5. Lauren has a paper route. She delivers papers to 35 homes every day. How many papers does she deliver in a week?

   _____ papers

1. $45 \times 5 =$ _____

   _____ $\div 5 = 45$

2. 
$$\begin{array}{r} 4\frac{6}{10} \\ -1\frac{3}{10} \\ \hline \end{array}$$
$$\begin{array}{r} 3\frac{2}{3} \\ -1\frac{1}{3} \\ \hline \end{array}$$

3. Circle the ways to make **54**.

   6 x 9     96 – 32     50 + 4

   100 ÷ 2     9 x 6     16 + 38

4. Which **two** units would be the best to measure the weight of an elephant?

   ○ kilograms     ○ grams

   ○ ounces     ○ pounds

5. How many are in:

   a day?     _____ hours

   a week?     _____ hours

1  43 x 8 = _____

2
```
   576
  -289
 ┌─────┐
 └─────┘
```
```
 ┌─────┐
 └─────┘
  +289
  576
```

3  Continue the pattern.

3  6  12  24  _____  _____  _____

4  Write the correct symbol in the circle.

    <   =   >

18 inches ◯ 2 feet

24 inches ◯ 2 feet

5  Julian sent party invitations to a dozen friends. The invitations cost $1.95 for a package of six. How much did Julian spend on invitations?

$_____

---

1  30 ÷ 8 = _____

(8 x 3) + 6 = _____

2
```
   426
  +393
 ┌─────┐
 └─────┘
```
```
 ┌─────┐
 └─────┘
  -426
  393
```

3  Write the number 1,962 in expanded form.

_____

4  If 96 ÷ 8 = 12, then 12 x 8 = _____.

5  Adrian is collecting newspapers to raise money. He collected 10 pounds of newspapers each day for 4 days and was paid 9¢ a pound. How much money did Adrian get for all the newspapers?

$_____

> ## Activity 1

Use the information on the map to solve the word problems.

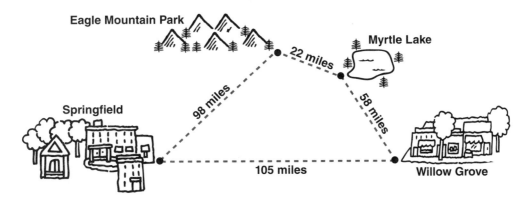

1. A food truck travels from Springfield to Willow Grove every day. Then it goes to Myrtle Lake, Eagle Mountain Park, and back to Springfield. How many miles does the truck travel each day?

    _____ miles

2. If the food truck holds enough gas to drive 190 miles, can the driver go to Eagle Mountain Park from Springfield without stopping for gas?

    ○ **yes**      ○ **no**

> ## Activity 2

1. Which figure has $\frac{2}{3}$ shaded?

2. On which number line does the arrow (↑) point to $\frac{2}{3}$?

1   106 – 17 = _____

2   128      308
    x   7    x   5

3   Color the rectangular prism.

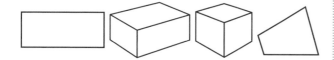

4   Write the correct symbol in the circle.

    <   =   >

    9,462  ◯  6,936

5   A train started with 826 people onboard. At the first stop, 93 people got off and 76 got on. How many people are on the train now?

    _____ people

1   4)‾56‾      5)‾60‾

2   980      The sum is an
    362      even number.
    + 659
             ◯ yes    ◯ no

3   For each number, circle the digit in the hundreds place. Draw an **X** on the digit in the ones place.

    8,320      14,608

4   How many ounces are in a pound?

    _____ ounces

5   How many of each coin would it take to make $2.00?

    _____ half dollars = $2.00

    _____ quarters = $2.00

    _____ dimes = $2.00

    _____ nickels = $2.00

1. $29 \times 3 =$ _____

   _____ $\div 3 = 29$

2.
   $\begin{array}{r} 9,063 \\ -\,4,135 \\ \hline \end{array}$     $\begin{array}{r} 8,624 \\ -\,6,809 \\ \hline \end{array}$

3. $\frac{1}{4}$ of $16 =$ _____

   Show your work.

4. What time is it?

   _____ minutes before _____

5. What number equals the centimeters in a meter minus the inches in a yard?

   _____

1. $90 \div 6 =$ _____

   $6 \times$ _____ $= 90$

2. Round 2,805 to the nearest thousand.

   _____

3. Write the number fifty thousand.

   _____

4. If $32 \div 8 = 4$, then $8 \times$ _____ $= 32$.

5. The farmer's prize pig has six piglets. One piglet weighs 8 pounds, four weigh 6 pounds each, and one weighs 5 pounds. What is the total weight of the piglets?

   _____ pounds

➤ **Activity 1**

Connect the letters below to make the following line segments:

| AB   BC   CD   DE   EF   FG   AF   BG   DG |

A ................. B

Which solid geometric figure did you make?

○ cube

F•               G•            •C

○ rectangular prism

○ hexagon

•            •
E            D

➤ **Activity 2**

**1 foot = 12 inches**

**1.** Mark the correct way to change five feet to inches.

   ○ 5 feet ÷ 1 foot = 5 inches

   ○ 5 feet x 12 inches = 60 inches

   ○ 5 feet + 12 inches = 17 inches

**1 pound = 16 ounces**

**2.** Mark the correct way to change three pounds to ounces.

   ○ 3 pounds + 16 ounces = 19 ounces

   ○ 16 pounds – 3 ounces = 13 ounces

   ○ 3 pounds x 16 ounces = 48 ounces

## TE Page 7 / SB Page 1

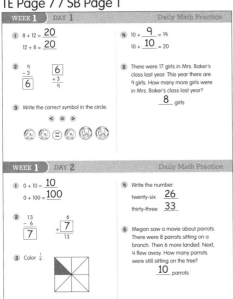

**WEEK 1 · DAY 1 — Daily Math Practice**

1. $8 + 12 = 20$
   $12 + 8 = 20$
2. $9 - 3 = 6$ ; $6 + 3 = 9$
3. Write the correct symbol in the circle. (< = >)
4. $10 + 9 = 19$
   $10 + 10 = 20$
5. There were 17 girls in Mrs. Baker's class last year. This year there are 9 girls. How many more girls were in Mrs. Baker's class last year? **8** girls

**WEEK 1 · DAY 2 — Daily Math Practice**

1. $0 + 10 = 10$
   $0 + 100 = 100$
2. $13 - 6 = 7$ ; $6 + 7 = 13$
3. Color $\frac{1}{8}$.
4. Write the number. twenty-six **26** ; thirty-three **33**
5. Megan saw a movie about parrots. There were 8 parrots sitting on a branch. Then 6 more landed. Next, 4 flew away. How many parrots were still sitting on the tree? **10** parrots

## TE Page 8 / SB Page 2

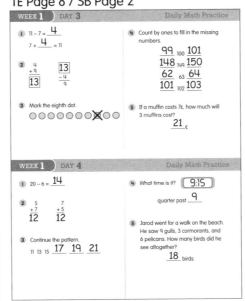

**WEEK 1 · DAY 3 — Daily Math Practice**

1. $11 - 7 = 4$
   $7 + 4 = 11$
2. $4 + 9 = 13$ ; $13 - 4 = 9$
3. Mark the eighth dot. (eighth dot marked with X)
4. Count by ones to fill in the missing numbers.
   99 **100** 101
   148 **149** 150
   62 **63** 64
   101 **102** 103
5. If a muffin costs 7¢, how much will 3 muffins cost? **21**¢

**WEEK 1 · DAY 4 — Daily Math Practice**

1. $20 - 6 = 14$
2. $5 + 7 = 12$ ; $7 + 5 = 12$
3. Continue the pattern. 11 13 15 **17 19 21**
4. What time is it? **9:15** quarter past **9**
5. Jarod went for a walk on the beach. He saw 9 gulls, 3 cormorants, and 6 pelicans. How many birds did he see altogether? **18** birds

## TE Page 9 / SB Page 3

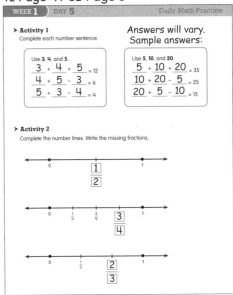

**WEEK 1 · DAY 5 — Daily Math Practice**

> **Activity 1**
Complete each number sentence.

Answers will vary. Sample answers:

Use 3, 4, and 5.
$3 + 4 + 5 = 12$
$4 + 5 - 3 = 6$
$5 + 3 - 4 = 4$

Use 5, 10, and 20.
$5 + 10 + 20 = 35$
$10 + 20 - 5 = 25$
$20 + 5 - 10 = 15$

> **Activity 2**
Complete the number lines. Write the missing fractions.
($\frac{1}{2}$, $\frac{3}{4}$, $\frac{2}{3}$)

## TE Page 10 / SB Page 4

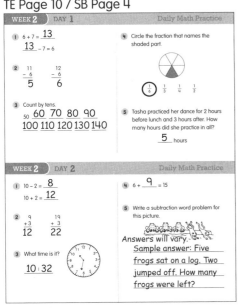

**WEEK 2 · DAY 1 — Daily Math Practice**

1. $6 + 7 = 13$
   $13 - 7 = 6$
2. $11 - 6 = 5$ ; $12 - 6 = 6$
3. Count by tens. 50 **60 70 80 90 100 110 120 130 140**
4. Circle the fraction that names the shaded part. ($\frac{1}{6}$)
5. Tasha practiced her dance for 2 hours before lunch and 3 hours after. How many hours did she practice in all? **5** hours

**WEEK 2 · DAY 2 — Daily Math Practice**

1. $10 - 2 = 8$
   $10 + 2 = 12$
2. $9 + 3 = 12$ ; $19 + 3 = 22$
3. What time is it? **10:32**
4. $6 + 9 = 15$
5. Write a subtraction word problem for this picture. Answers will vary. Sample answer: Five frogs sat on a log. Two jumped off. How many frogs were left?

## TE Page 11 / SB Page 5

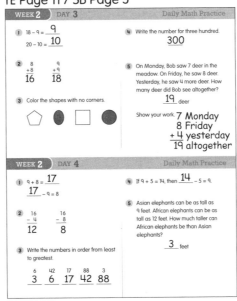

**WEEK 2 · DAY 3 — Daily Math Practice**

1. $18 - 9 = 9$
   $20 - 10 = 10$
2. $8 + 8 = 16$ ; $9 + 9 = 18$
3. Color the shapes with no corners.
4. Write the number for three hundred. **300**
5. On Monday, Bob saw 7 deer in the meadow. On Friday, he saw 8 deer. Yesterday, he saw 4 more deer. How many deer did Bob see altogether? **19** deer
   Show your work. 7 Monday / 8 Friday / + 4 yesterday / 19 altogether

**WEEK 2 · DAY 4 — Daily Math Practice**

1. $9 + 8 = 17$
   $17 - 9 = 8$
2. $16 - 4 = 12$ ; $16 - 8 = 8$
3. Write the numbers in order from least to greatest. 6 42 17 88 3 → **3 6 17 42 88**
4. If $9 + 5 = 14$, then **14** $- 5 = 9$.
5. Asian elephants can be as tall as 9 feet. African elephants can be as tall as 12 feet. How much taller can African elephants be than Asian elephants? **3** feet

## TE Page 12 / SB Page 6

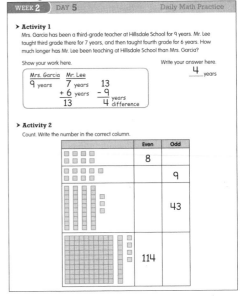

**WEEK 2 · DAY 5 — Daily Math Practice**

> **Activity 1**
Mrs. Garcia has been a third-grade teacher at Hillsdale School for 9 years. Mr. Lee taught third grade there for 7 years, and then taught fourth grade for 6 years. How much longer has Mr. Lee been teaching at Hillsdale School than Mrs. Garcia?

Show your work here.
| Mrs. Garcia | Mr. Lee |
|---|---|
| 9 years | 7 years / + 6 years / 13 |
| | 13 / − 9 / 4 difference |

Write your answer here. **4** years

> **Activity 2**
Count. Write the number in the correct column.

| | Even | Odd |
|---|---|---|
| | 8 | |
| | | 9 |
| | | 43 |
| | 114 | |

## TE Page 13 / SB Page 7

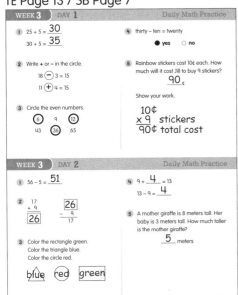

**WEEK 3 · DAY 1 — Daily Math Practice**

1. $25 + 5 = 30$
   $30 + 5 = 35$
2. Write + or − in the circle. $18 - 3 = 15$ ; $11 + 4 = 15$
3. Circle the even numbers. **6** 9 **12** 43 **36** 65
4. thirty − ten = twenty ● yes  ○ no
5. Rainbow stickers cost 10¢ each. How much will it cost Jill to buy 9 stickers? **90**¢
   Show your work. 10¢ × 9 stickers = 90¢ total cost

**WEEK 3 · DAY 2 — Daily Math Practice**

1. $56 - 5 = 51$
2. $17 + 9 = 26$ ; $26 - 9 = 17$
3. Color the rectangle green. Color the triangle blue. Color the circle red. **blue red green**
4. $9 + 4 = 13$ ; $13 - 9 = 4$
5. A mother giraffe is 8 meters tall. Her baby is 3 meters tall. How much taller is the mother giraffe? **5** meters

## TE Page 14 / SB Page 8

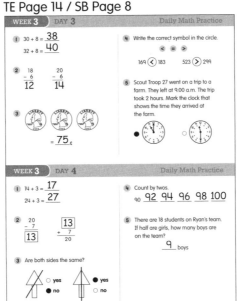

**WEEK 3 · DAY 3 — Daily Math Practice**

1. $30 + 8 = 38$
   $32 + 8 = 40$
2. $18 - 6 = 12$ ; $20 - 6 = 14$
3. (coins) = **75**¢
4. Write the correct symbol in the circle. (< = >)
   169 **<** 183    523 **>** 299
5. Scout Troop 27 went on a trip to a farm. They left at 9:00 a.m. The trip took 2 hours. Mark the clock that shows the time they arrived at the farm. (first clock marked)

**WEEK 3 · DAY 4 — Daily Math Practice**

1. $14 + 3 = 17$
   $24 + 3 = 27$
2. $20 - 7 = 13$ ; $13 + 7 = 20$
3. Are both sides the same? (left: ○ yes ● no) (right: ● yes ○ no)
4. Count by twos. 90 **92 94 96 98 100**
5. There are 18 students on Ryan's team. If half are girls, how many boys are on the team? **9** boys

## TE Page 15 / SB Page 9

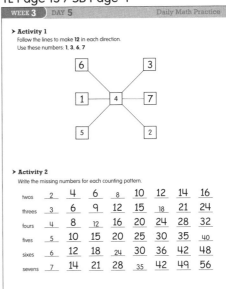

**WEEK 3 · DAY 5 — Daily Math Practice**

> **Activity 1**
Follow the lines to make 12 in each direction. Use these numbers: 1, 3, 6, 7
(6, 3 / 1, 4, 7 / 5, 2)

> **Activity 2**
Write the missing numbers for each counting pattern.

| twos | 2 | **4** | 6 | 8 | **10** | 12 | **14** | **16** |
|---|---|---|---|---|---|---|---|---|
| threes | 3 | **6** | **9** | 12 | 15 | **18** | **21** | **24** |
| fours | 4 | **8** | 12 | **16** | 20 | **24** | **28** | **32** |
| fives | 5 | **10** | 15 | **20** | 25 | **30** | 35 | **40** |
| sixes | 6 | **12** | 18 | **24** | 30 | **36** | **42** | **48** |
| sevens | 7 | **14** | 21 | **28** | 35 | **42** | **49** | **56** |

## TE Page 16 / SB Page 10

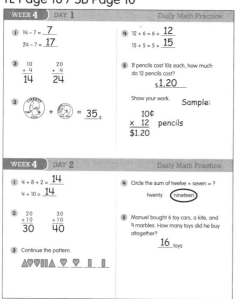

**WEEK 4 DAY 1** — Daily Math Practice

1. $14 - 7 = \underline{7}$
   $24 - 7 = \underline{17}$

2. $\begin{array}{r} 10 \\ + 4 \\ \hline 14 \end{array}$  $\begin{array}{r} 20 \\ + 4 \\ \hline 24 \end{array}$

3. 🪙 + 🪙 = $\underline{35}$¢

4. $12 + 6 = 6 + \underline{12}$
   $15 + 5 = 5 + \underline{15}$

5. If pencils cost 10¢ each, how much do 12 pencils cost? $\underline{\$1.20}$

   Show your work.   **Sample:**
   $\begin{array}{r} 10¢ \\ \times\ 12 \\ \hline \$1.20 \end{array}$ pencils

**WEEK 4 DAY 2** — Daily Math Practice

1. $4 + 8 + 2 = \underline{14}$
   $4 + 10 = \underline{14}$

2. $\begin{array}{r} 20 \\ +10 \\ \hline 30 \end{array}$  $\begin{array}{r} 30 \\ +10 \\ \hline 40 \end{array}$

3. Continue the pattern.
   ▲▽▯▮ ♡ ♡ ▯ ▮

4. Circle the sum of twelve + seven = ?
   twenty   (nineteen)

5. Manuel bought 6 toy cars, a kite, and 9 marbles. How many toys did he buy altogether?
   $\underline{16}$ toys

## TE Page 17 / SB Page 11

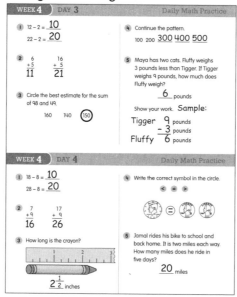

**WEEK 4 DAY 3** — Daily Math Practice

1. $12 - 2 = \underline{10}$
   $22 - 2 = \underline{20}$

2. $\begin{array}{r} 6 \\ +5 \\ \hline 11 \end{array}$  $\begin{array}{r} 16 \\ +5 \\ \hline 21 \end{array}$

3. Circle the best estimate for the sum of 98 and 49.
   160   140   (150)

4. Continue the pattern.
   100  200  $\underline{300}$  $\underline{400}$  $\underline{500}$

5. Maya has two cats. Fluffy weighs 3 pounds less than Tigger. If Tigger weighs 9 pounds, how much does Fluffy weigh?
   $\underline{6}$ pounds

   Show your work.   **Sample:**
   Tigger $\underline{9}$ pounds
   $-\underline{3}$ pounds
   Fluffy $\underline{6}$ pounds

**WEEK 4 DAY 4** — Daily Math Practice

1. $18 - 8 = \underline{10}$
   $28 - 8 = \underline{20}$

2. $\begin{array}{r} 7 \\ +9 \\ \hline 16 \end{array}$  $\begin{array}{r} 17 \\ +9 \\ \hline 26 \end{array}$

3. How long is the crayon?
   $2\frac{1}{2}$ inches

4. Write the correct symbol in the circle.
   <   =   >
   🪙🪙 (=) 🪙🪙

5. Jamal rides his bike to school and back home. It is two miles each way. How many miles does he ride in five days?
   $\underline{20}$ miles

## TE Page 18 / SB Page 12

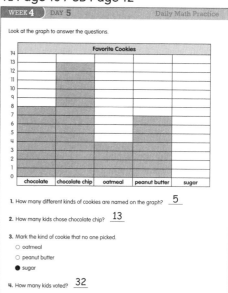

**WEEK 4 DAY 5** — Daily Math Practice

Look at the graph to answer the questions.

**Favorite Cookies**

(bar graph: chocolate = 8, chocolate chip = 13, oatmeal = 6, peanut butter = 5, sugar = 0)

1. How many different kinds of cookies are named on the graph? $\underline{5}$
2. How many kids chose chocolate chip? $\underline{13}$
3. Mark the kind of cookie that no one picked.
   ○ oatmeal
   ○ peanut butter
   ● sugar
4. How many kids voted? $\underline{32}$

## TE Page 19 / SB Page 13

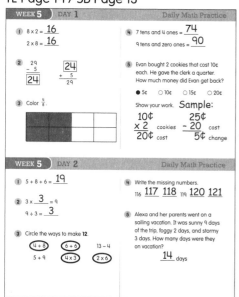

**WEEK 5 DAY 1** — Daily Math Practice

1. $8 \times 2 = \underline{16}$
   $2 \times 8 = \underline{16}$

2. $\begin{array}{r} 29 \\ -5 \\ \hline \boxed{24} \end{array}$  $\begin{array}{r} \boxed{24} \\ +5 \\ \hline 29 \end{array}$

3. Color $\frac{4}{8}$.

4. 7 tens and 4 ones $\underline{74}$
   9 tens and zero ones $\underline{90}$

5. Evan bought 2 cookies that cost 10¢ each. He gave the clerk a quarter. How much money did Evan get back?
   ● 5¢   ○ 10¢   ○ 15¢   ○ 20¢

   Show your work.   **Sample:**
   $\begin{array}{r} 10¢ \\ \times 2 \\ \hline 20¢ \end{array}$ cookies   $\begin{array}{r} 25¢ \\ -20 \\ \hline 5¢ \end{array}$ change
   cost   cost

**WEEK 5 DAY 2** — Daily Math Practice

1. $5 + 8 + 6 = \underline{19}$

2. $3 \times \underline{3} = 9$
   $9 \div 3 = \underline{3}$

3. Circle the ways to make 12.
   (4+8)   (6+6)   13 - 4
   5 + 9   (4×3)   (2×6)

4. Write the missing numbers.
   116  $\underline{117}$  $\underline{118}$  119  $\underline{120}$  $\underline{121}$

5. Alexa and her parents went on a sailing vacation. It was sunny 9 days of the trip, foggy 2 days, and stormy 3 days. How many days were they on vacation?
   $\underline{14}$ days

## TE Page 20 / SB Page 14

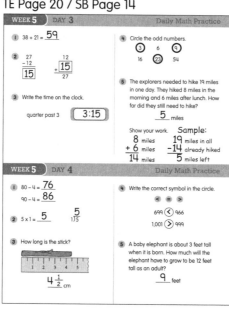

**WEEK 5 DAY 3** — Daily Math Practice

1. $38 + 21 = \underline{59}$

2. $\begin{array}{r} 27 \\ -12 \\ \hline \boxed{15} \end{array}$  $\begin{array}{r} \boxed{15} \\ +12 \\ \hline 27 \end{array}$

3. Write the time on the clock.
   quarter past 3   [3:15]

4. Circle the odd numbers.
   (3)  6  (9)
   16  (23)  54

5. The explorers needed to hike 19 miles in one day. They hiked 8 miles in the morning and 6 miles after lunch. How far did they still need to hike?
   $\underline{5}$ miles

   Show your work.   **Sample:**
   $\begin{array}{r} 8 \text{ miles} \\ +6 \text{ miles} \\ \hline 14 \text{ miles} \end{array}$   $\begin{array}{r} 19 \text{ miles in all} \\ -14 \text{ already hiked} \\ \hline 5 \text{ miles left} \end{array}$

**WEEK 5 DAY 4** — Daily Math Practice

1. $80 - 4 = \underline{76}$
   $90 - 4 = \underline{86}$

2. $5 \times 1 = \underline{5}$   $\begin{array}{r} 5 \\ \hline 1)5 \end{array}$

3. How long is the stick?
   $4\frac{1}{2}$ cm

4. Write the correct symbol in the circle.
   <   =   >
   $699 (<) 966$
   $1,001 (>) 999$

5. A baby elephant is about 3 feet tall when it is born. How much will the elephant have to grow to be 12 feet tall as an adult?
   $\underline{9}$ feet

## TE Page 21 / SB Page 15

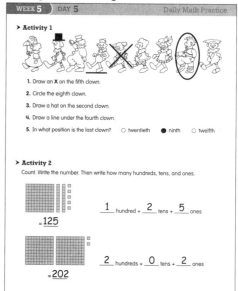

**WEEK 5 DAY 5** — Daily Math Practice

➤ **Activity 1**

1. Draw an **X** on the fifth clown.
2. Circle the eighth clown.
3. Draw a hat on the second clown.
4. Draw a line under the fourth clown.
5. In what position is the last clown?   ○ twentieth   ● ninth   ○ twelfth

➤ **Activity 2**

Count. Write the number. Then write how many hundreds, tens, and ones.

$= \underline{125}$   $\underline{1}$ hundred + $\underline{2}$ tens + $\underline{5}$ ones

$= \underline{202}$   $\underline{2}$ hundreds + $\underline{0}$ tens + $\underline{2}$ ones

## TE Page 22 / SB Page 16

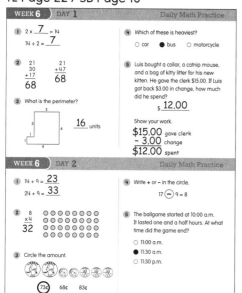

**WEEK 6 DAY 1** — Daily Math Practice

1. $2 \times \underline{7} = 14$
   $14 \div 2 = \underline{7}$

2. $\begin{array}{r} 21 \\ 30 \\ +17 \\ \hline 68 \end{array}$  $\begin{array}{r} 21 \\ +47 \\ \hline 68 \end{array}$

3. What is the perimeter?
   $\underline{16}$ units

4. Which of these is heaviest?
   ○ car   ● bus   ○ motorcycle

5. Luis bought a collar, a catnip mouse, and a bag of kitty litter for his new kitten. He gave the clerk $15.00. If Luis got back $3.00 in change, how much did he spend?
   $\underline{\$12.00}$

   Show your work.
   $\begin{array}{r} \$15.00 \text{ gave clerk} \\ -3.00 \text{ change} \\ \hline \$12.00 \text{ spent} \end{array}$

**WEEK 6 DAY 2** — Daily Math Practice

1. $14 + 9 = \underline{23}$
   $24 + 9 = \underline{33}$

2. $\begin{array}{r} 8 \\ 32 \end{array}$ (circles)

3. Circle the amount.
   (73¢)   68¢   83¢

## TE Page 23 / SB Page 17

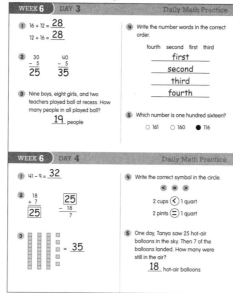

**WEEK 6 DAY 3** — Daily Math Practice

1. $16 + 12 = \underline{28}$
   $12 + 16 = \underline{28}$

2. $\begin{array}{r} 30 \\ -5 \\ \hline 25 \end{array}$  $\begin{array}{r} 40 \\ -5 \\ \hline 35 \end{array}$

3. Nine boys, eight girls, and two teachers played ball at recess. How many people in all played ball?
   $\underline{19}$ people

4. Write the number words in the correct order.
   fourth  second  first  third
   $\underline{first}$
   $\underline{second}$
   $\underline{third}$
   $\underline{fourth}$

5. Which number is one hundred sixteen?
   ○ 161   ○ 160   ● 116

**WEEK 6 DAY 4** — Daily Math Practice

1. $41 - 9 = \underline{32}$

2. $\begin{array}{r} 18 \\ +7 \\ \hline \boxed{25} \end{array}$  $\begin{array}{r} \boxed{25} \\ -18 \\ \hline 7 \end{array}$

3. (blocks) $= \underline{35}$

4. Write the correct symbol in the circle.
   <   =   >
   2 cups (<) 1 quart
   2 pints (=) 1 quart

5. One day, Tanya saw 25 hot-air balloons in the sky. Then 7 of the balloons landed. How many were still in the air?
   $\underline{18}$ hot-air balloons

## TE Page 24 / SB Page 18

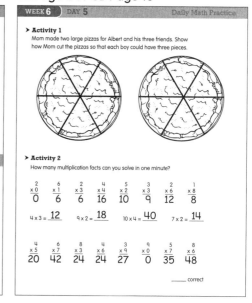

**WEEK 6 DAY 5** — Daily Math Practice

➤ **Activity 1**

Mom made two large pizzas for Albert and his three friends. Show how Mom cut the pizzas so that each boy could have three pieces.

➤ **Activity 2**

How many multiplication facts can you solve in one minute?

$\begin{array}{r} 2 \\ \times 0 \\ \hline 0 \end{array}$ $\begin{array}{r} 6 \\ \times 1 \\ \hline 6 \end{array}$ $\begin{array}{r} 2 \\ \times 3 \\ \hline 16 \end{array}$ $\begin{array}{r} 4 \\ \times 4 \\ \hline 16 \end{array}$ $\begin{array}{r} 5 \\ \times 2 \\ \hline 10 \end{array}$ $\begin{array}{r} 3 \\ \times 3 \\ \hline 9 \end{array}$ $\begin{array}{r} 2 \\ \times 6 \\ \hline 12 \end{array}$ $\begin{array}{r} 1 \\ \times 8 \\ \hline 8 \end{array}$

$4 \times 3 = \underline{12}$   $9 \times 2 = \underline{18}$   $10 \times 4 = \underline{40}$   $7 \times 2 = \underline{14}$

$\begin{array}{r} 4 \\ \times 5 \\ \hline 20 \end{array}$ $\begin{array}{r} 6 \\ \times 7 \\ \hline 42 \end{array}$ $\begin{array}{r} 8 \\ \times 3 \\ \hline 24 \end{array}$ $\begin{array}{r} 4 \\ \times 6 \\ \hline 24 \end{array}$ $\begin{array}{r} 3 \\ \times 9 \\ \hline 27 \end{array}$ $\begin{array}{r} 2 \\ \times 0 \\ \hline 0 \end{array}$ $\begin{array}{r} 5 \\ \times 7 \\ \hline 35 \end{array}$ $\begin{array}{r} 8 \\ \times 6 \\ \hline 48 \end{array}$

_____ correct

## TE Page 25 / SB Page 19

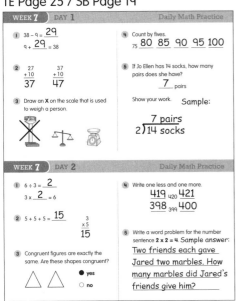

**WEEK 7 — DAY 1** — Daily Math Practice

1. 38 − 9 = **29**
   9 + **29** = 38

2. 27 +10 = **37**   37 +10 = **47**

3. Draw an **X** on the scale that is used to weigh a person.

4. Count by fives.
   75 **80 85 90 95 100**

5. If Jo Ellen has 14 socks, how many pairs does she have?
   **7** pairs
   Show your work. **Sample:**
   7 pairs
   2)14 socks

**WEEK 7 — DAY 2** — Daily Math Practice

1. 6 ÷ 3 = **2**
   3 × **2** = 6

2. 5 + 5 + 5 = **15**    3 ×5 **15**

3. Congruent figures are exactly the same. Are these shapes congruent?
   ● yes
   ○ no

4. Write one less and one more.
   **419** 420 **421**
   **398** 399 **400**

5. Write a word problem for the number sentence **2 × 2 = 4**. **Sample answer:**
   Two friends each gave Jared two marbles. How many marbles did Jared's friends give him?

## TE Page 26 / SB Page 20

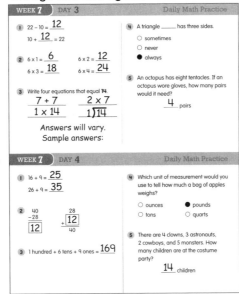

**WEEK 7 — DAY 3** — Daily Math Practice

1. 22 − 10 = **12**
   10 + **12** = 22

2. 6 × 1 = **6**    6 × 2 = **12**
   6 × 3 = **18**    6 × 4 = **24**

3. Write four equations that equal **14.**
   7 + 7    2 × 7
   1 × 14   1)14
   Answers will vary.
   Sample answers:

**WEEK 7 — DAY 4** — Daily Math Practice

1. 16 + 9 = **25**
   26 + 9 = **35**

2. 40 −28 **12**    28 +12 **40**

3. 1 hundred + 6 tens + 9 ones = **169**

4. A triangle ____ has three sides.
   ○ sometimes
   ○ never
   ● always

5. An octopus has eight tentacles. If an octopus wore gloves, how many pairs would it need?
   **4** pairs

4. Which unit of measurement would you use to tell how much a bag of apples weighs?
   ○ ounces   ● pounds
   ○ tons     ○ quarts

5. There are 4 clowns, 3 astronauts, 2 cowboys, and 5 monsters. How many children are at the costume party?
   **14** children

## TE Page 27 / SB Page 21

**WEEK 7 — DAY 5** — Daily Math Practice

**➤ Activity 1**
Fill in the boxes.

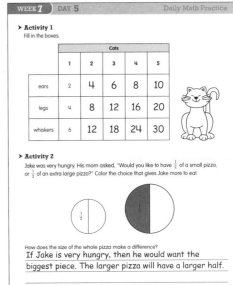

| Cats | 1 | 2 | 3 | 4 | 5 |
|---|---|---|---|---|---|
| ears | 2 | **4** | **6** | **8** | **10** |
| legs | 4 | **8** | **12** | **16** | **20** |
| whiskers | 6 | **12** | **18** | **24** | **30** |

**➤ Activity 2**
Jake was very hungry. His mom asked, "Would you like to have $\frac{1}{2}$ of a small pizza, or $\frac{1}{2}$ of an extra large pizza?" Color the choice that gives Jake more to eat.

How does the size of the whole pizza make a difference?
If Jake is very hungry, then he would want the biggest piece. The larger pizza will have a larger half.

## TE Page 28 / SB Page 22

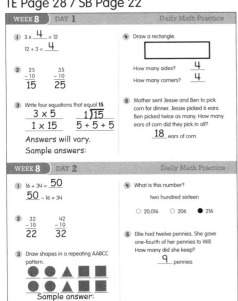

**WEEK 8 — DAY 1** — Daily Math Practice

1. 3 × **4** = 12
   12 ÷ 3 = **4**

2. 25 −10 **15**    35 −10 **25**

3. Write four equations that equal **15.**
   3 × 5     1)15
   1 × 15    5 + 5 + 5
   Answers will vary.
   Sample answers:

**WEEK 8 — DAY 2** — Daily Math Practice

1. 16 + 34 = **50**
   **50** − 16 = 34

2. 32 −10 **22**    42 −10 **32**

3. Draw shapes in a repeating AABCC pattern.
   Sample answer:

4. Draw a rectangle.
   How many sides? **4**
   How many corners? **4**

5. Mother sent Jessie and Ben to pick corn for dinner. Jessie picked 6 ears. Ben picked twice as many. How many ears of corn did they pick in all?
   **18** ears of corn

4. What is this number?
   two hundred sixteen
   ○ 20,016   ○ 206   ● 216

5. Ellie had twelve pennies. She gave one-fourth of her pennies to Will. How many did she keep?
   **9** pennies

## TE Page 29 / SB Page 23

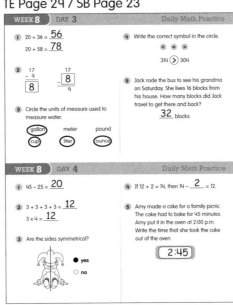

**WEEK 8 — DAY 3** — Daily Math Practice

1. 20 + 36 = **56**
   20 + 58 = **78**

2. 17 −9 **8**    17 −**8** **9**

3. Circle the units of measure used to measure water.
   (gallon)  meter  pound
   (cup)  (liter)  (ounce)

**WEEK 8 — DAY 4** — Daily Math Practice

1. 45 − 25 = **20**

2. 3 + 3 + 3 + 3 = **12**
   3 × 4 = **12**

3. Are the sides symmetrical?
   ● yes
   ○ no

4. Write the correct symbol in the circle.
   < = >
   314 (>) 304

5. Jack rode the bus to see his grandma on Saturday. She lives 16 blocks from his house. How many blocks did Jack travel to get there and back?
   **32** blocks

4. If 12 + 2 = 14, then 14 − **2** = 12.

5. Amy made a cake for a family picnic. The cake had to bake for 45 minutes. Amy put it in the oven at 2:00 p.m. Write the time that she took the cake out of the oven.
   **2:45**

## TE Page 30 / SB Page 24

**WEEK 8 — DAY 5** — Daily Math Practice

Morgan asked her friends what kinds of pets they have. Record their answers on the graph. Then answer the questions about the graph.

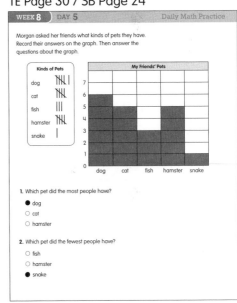

**Kinds of Pets**
dog — |||| ||
cat — ||||
fish — |||
hamster — ||||
snake — |

1. Which pet did the most people have?
   ● dog
   ○ cat
   ○ hamster

2. Which pet did the fewest people have?
   ○ fish
   ○ hamster
   ● snake

## TE Page 31 / SB Page 25

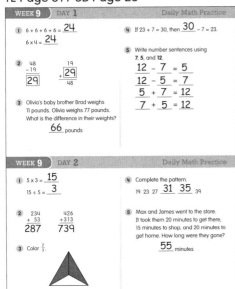

**WEEK 9 — DAY 1** — Daily Math Practice

1. 6 + 6 + 6 + 6 = **24**
   6 × 4 = **24**

2. 48 −19 **29**    19 +**29** **48**

3. Olivia's baby brother Brad weighs 11 pounds. Olivia weighs 77 pounds. What is the difference in their weights?
   **66** pounds

**WEEK 9 — DAY 2** — Daily Math Practice

1. 5 × 3 = **15**
   15 ÷ 5 = **3**

2. 234 + 53 **287**    426 +313 **739**

3. Color $\frac{2}{3}$.

4. If 23 + 7 = 30, then **30** − 7 = 23.

5. Write number sentences using **7, 5,** and **12.**
   12 − 7 = 5
   12 − 5 = 7
   5 + 7 = 12
   7 + 5 = 12

4. Complete the pattern.
   19 23 27 **31 35** 39

5. Max and James went to the store. It took them 20 minutes to get there, 15 minutes to shop, and 20 minutes to get home. How long were they gone?
   **55** minutes

## TE Page 32 / SB Page 26

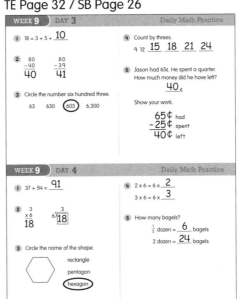

**WEEK 9 — DAY 3** — Daily Math Practice

1. 18 = 3 + 5 + **10**

2. 80 −40 **40**    80 −39 **41**

3. Circle the number six hundred three.
   63   630   (603)   6,300

**WEEK 9 — DAY 4** — Daily Math Practice

1. 37 + 54 = **91**

2. 3 ×6 **18**    6)**18**

3. Circle the name of the shape.
   rectangle
   pentagon
   (hexagon)

4. Count by threes.
   9 12 **15 18 21 24**

5. Jason had 65¢. He spent a quarter. How much money did he have left?
   **40**¢
   Show your work.
   65¢ had
   −25¢ spent
   40¢ left

4. 2 × 6 = 6 × **2**
   3 × 6 = 6 × **3**

5. How many bagels?
   $\frac{1}{2}$ dozen = **6** bagels
   2 dozen = **24** bagels

## TE Page 33 / SB Page 27

**WEEK 9 — DAY 5** — Daily Math Practice

Look at the calendar to answer the questions.

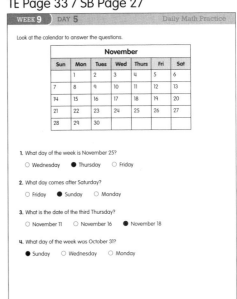

**November**

| Sun | Mon | Tues | Wed | Thurs | Fri | Sat |
|---|---|---|---|---|---|---|
|  |  | 1 | 2 | 3 | 4 | 5 | 6 |
| 7 | 8 | 9 | 10 | 11 | 12 | 13 |
| 14 | 15 | 16 | 17 | 18 | 19 | 20 |
| 21 | 22 | 23 | 24 | 25 | 26 | 27 |
| 28 | 29 | 30 |  |  |  |  |

1. What day of the week is November 25?
   ○ Wednesday   ● Thursday   ○ Friday

2. What day comes after Saturday?
   ○ Friday   ● Sunday   ○ Monday

3. What is the date of the third Thursday?
   ○ November 11   ○ November 16   ● November 18

4. What day of the week was October 31?
   ● Sunday   ○ Wednesday   ○ Monday

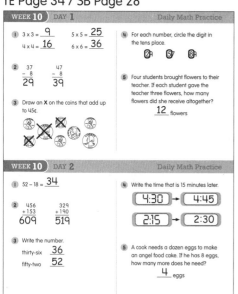

**WEEK 10 DAY 1** — Daily Math Practice

1. $3 \times 3 = $ 9  $5 \times 5 = $ 25
   $4 \times 4 = $ 16  $6 \times 6 = $ 36

2. $\begin{array}{r} 37 \\ -8 \\ \hline 29 \end{array}$  $\begin{array}{r} 47 \\ -8 \\ \hline 39 \end{array}$

3. Draw an **X** on the coins that add up to 45¢.

4. For each number, circle the digit in the tens place.
   (2)1  (5)7  (8)1

5. Four students brought flowers to their teacher. If each student gave the teacher three flowers, how many flowers did she receive altogether?
   12 flowers

**WEEK 10 DAY 2** — Daily Math Practice

1. $52 - 18 = $ 34

2. $\begin{array}{r} 456 \\ +153 \\ \hline 609 \end{array}$  $\begin{array}{r} 329 \\ +190 \\ \hline 519 \end{array}$

3. Write the number.
   thirty-six  36
   fifty-two  52

4. Write the time that is 15 minutes later.
   4:30 → 4:45
   2:15 → 2:30

5. A cook needs a dozen eggs to make an angel food cake. If he has 8 eggs, how many more does he need?
   4 eggs

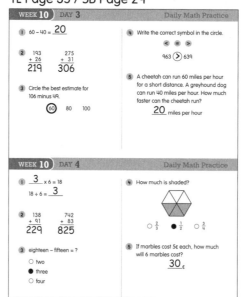

**WEEK 10 DAY 3** — Daily Math Practice

1. $60 - 40 = $ 20

2. $\begin{array}{r} 193 \\ +26 \\ \hline 219 \end{array}$  $\begin{array}{r} 275 \\ +31 \\ \hline 306 \end{array}$

3. Circle the best estimate for 106 minus 49.
   (60)  80  100

4. Write the correct symbol in the circle.
   $963 \; (>) \; 639$

5. A cheetah can run 60 miles per hour for a short distance. A greyhound dog can run 40 miles per hour. How much faster can the cheetah run?
   20 miles per hour

**WEEK 10 DAY 4** — Daily Math Practice

1. $3 \times 6 = 18$
   $18 \div 6 = $ 3

2. $\begin{array}{r} 138 \\ +91 \\ \hline 229 \end{array}$  $\begin{array}{r} 742 \\ +83 \\ \hline 825 \end{array}$

3. eighteen − fifteen = ?
   ○ two
   ● three
   ○ four

4. How much is shaded?
   ○ $\frac{2}{3}$  ● $\frac{1}{2}$  ○ $\frac{3}{4}$

5. If marbles cost 5¢ each, how much will 6 marbles cost?
   30 ¢

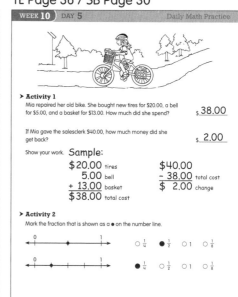

**WEEK 10 DAY 5** — Daily Math Practice

**Activity 1**

Mia repaired her old bike. She bought new tires for $20.00, a bell for $5.00, and a basket for $13.00. How much did she spend?
$ 38.00

If Mia gave the salesclerk $40.00, how much money did she get back?
$ 2.00

Show your work.  Sample:
$\begin{array}{r} \$20.00 \text{ tires} \\ 5.00 \text{ bell} \\ +13.00 \text{ basket} \\ \hline \$38.00 \text{ total cost} \end{array}$   $\begin{array}{r} \$40.00 \\ -38.00 \text{ total cost} \\ \hline \$\;2.00 \text{ change} \end{array}$

**Activity 2**
Mark the fraction that is shown as a ● on the number line.

○ $\frac{1}{4}$  ● $\frac{1}{2}$  ○ 1  ○ $\frac{1}{8}$

● $\frac{1}{4}$  ○ $\frac{1}{2}$  ○ 1  ○ $\frac{1}{8}$

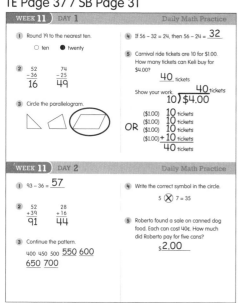

**WEEK 11 DAY 1** — Daily Math Practice

1. Round 19 to the nearest ten.
   ○ ten  ● twenty

2. $\begin{array}{r} 52 \\ -36 \\ \hline 16 \end{array}$  $\begin{array}{r} 74 \\ -25 \\ \hline 49 \end{array}$

3. Circle the parallelogram.

4. If $56 - 32 = 24$, then $56 - 24 = $ 32

5. Carnival ride tickets are 10 for $1.00. How many tickets can Keli buy for $4.00?
   40 tickets
   Show your work.  40 tickets
   $10)\overline{\$4.00}$
   ($1.00) 10 tickets
   OR ($1.00) 10 tickets
   ($1.00) 10 tickets
   ($1.00) +10 tickets
   40 tickets

**WEEK 11 DAY 2** — Daily Math Practice

1. $93 - 36 = $ 57

2. $\begin{array}{r} 52 \\ +39 \\ \hline 91 \end{array}$  $\begin{array}{r} 28 \\ +16 \\ \hline 44 \end{array}$

3. Continue the pattern.
   400 450 500 550 600 650 700

4. Write the correct symbol in the circle.
   $5 \; (\times) \; 7 = 35$

5. Roberto found a sale on canned dog food. Each can cost 40¢. How much did Roberto pay for five cans?
   $ 2.00

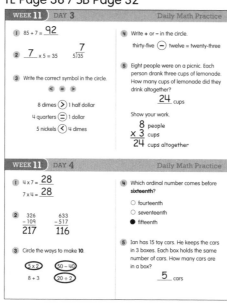

**WEEK 11 DAY 3** — Daily Math Practice

1. $85 + 7 = $ 92

2. $7 \times 5 = 35$   $5)\overline{35}$  7

3. Write the correct symbol in the circle.
   8 dimes $(>)$ 1 half dollar
   4 quarters $(=)$ 1 dollar
   5 nickels $(<)$ 4 dimes

4. Write + or − in the circle.
   thirty-five $(-)$ twelve = twenty-three

5. Eight people were on a picnic. Each person drank three cups of lemonade. How many cups of lemonade did they drink altogether?
   24 cups
   Show your work.
   $\begin{array}{r} 8 \text{ people} \\ \times 3 \text{ cups} \\ \hline 24 \text{ cups altogether} \end{array}$

**WEEK 11 DAY 4** — Daily Math Practice

1. $4 \times 7 = $ 28
   $7 \times 4 = $ 28

2. $\begin{array}{r} 326 \\ -109 \\ \hline 217 \end{array}$  $\begin{array}{r} 633 \\ -517 \\ \hline 116 \end{array}$

3. Circle the ways to make 10.
   (5 × 2)  (50 − 40)
   8 + 3  (20 ÷ 2)

4. Which ordinal number comes before **sixteenth**?
   ○ fourteenth
   ○ seventeenth
   ● fifteenth

5. Ian has 15 toy cars. He keeps the cars in 3 boxes. Each box holds the same number of cars. How many cars are in a box?
   5 cars

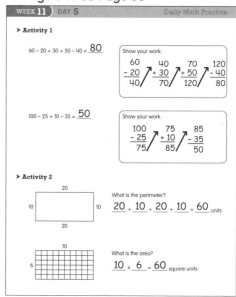

**WEEK 11 DAY 5** — Daily Math Practice

**Activity 1**

$60 - 20 + 30 + 50 - 40 = $ 80
Show your work.
$\begin{array}{r} 60 \\ -20 \\ \hline 40 \end{array} \nearrow \begin{array}{r} 40 \\ +30 \\ \hline 70 \end{array} \nearrow \begin{array}{r} 70 \\ +50 \\ \hline 120 \end{array} \searrow \begin{array}{r} 120 \\ -40 \\ \hline 80 \end{array}$

$100 - 25 + 10 - 35 = $ 50
Show your work.
$\begin{array}{r} 100 \\ -25 \\ \hline 75 \end{array} \nearrow \begin{array}{r} 75 \\ +10 \\ \hline 85 \end{array} \searrow \begin{array}{r} 85 \\ -35 \\ \hline 50 \end{array}$

**Activity 2**

What is the perimeter?
$20 + 10 + 20 + 10 = 60$ units

What is the area?
$10 \times 6 = 60$ square units

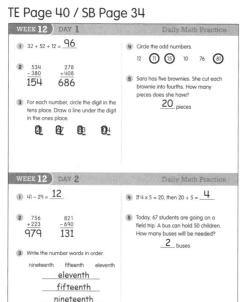

**WEEK 12 DAY 1** — Daily Math Practice

1. $32 + 52 + 12 = $ 96

2. $\begin{array}{r} 534 \\ -380 \\ \hline 154 \end{array}$  $\begin{array}{r} 278 \\ +408 \\ \hline 686 \end{array}$

3. For each number, circle the digit in the tens place. Draw a line under the digit in the ones place.
   (7)<u>4</u>  (2)<u>9</u>  (8)<u>3</u>  (0)<u>4</u>

4. Circle the odd numbers.
   12  (11)  (15)  10  76  (81)

5. Sara has five brownies. She cut each brownie into fourths. How many pieces does she have?
   20 pieces

**WEEK 12 DAY 2** — Daily Math Practice

1. $41 - 29 = $ 12

2. $\begin{array}{r} 756 \\ +223 \\ \hline 979 \end{array}$  $\begin{array}{r} 821 \\ -690 \\ \hline 131 \end{array}$

3. Write the number words in order.
   nineteenth  fifteenth  eleventh
   eleventh
   fifteenth
   nineteenth

4. If $4 \times 5 = 20$, then $20 \div 5 = $ 4

5. Today, 67 students are going on a field trip. A bus can hold 50 children. How many buses will be needed?
   2 buses

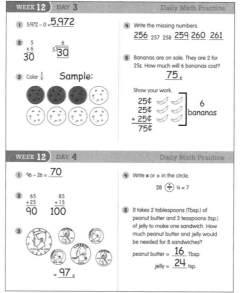

**WEEK 12 DAY 3** — Daily Math Practice

1. $5,972 - 0 = $ 5,972

2. $\begin{array}{r} 5 \\ \times 6 \\ \hline 30 \end{array}$   $5)\overline{30}$  6

3. Color $\frac{3}{8}$.  Sample:

4. Write the missing numbers.
   256 257 258 259 260 261

5. Bananas are on sale. They are 2 for 25¢. How much will 6 bananas cost?
   75 ¢
   Show your work.
   $\begin{array}{r} 25¢ \\ 25¢ \\ +25¢ \\ \hline 75¢ \end{array}$   6 bananas

**WEEK 12 DAY 4** — Daily Math Practice

1. $96 - 26 = $ 70

2. $\begin{array}{r} 65 \\ +25 \\ \hline 90 \end{array}$  $\begin{array}{r} 85 \\ +15 \\ \hline 100 \end{array}$

3. = 97 ¢

4. Write × or ÷ in the circle.
   $28 \; (\div) \; 4 = 7$

5. It takes 2 tablespoons (Tbsp.) of peanut butter and 3 teaspoons (tsp.) of jelly to make one sandwich. How much peanut butter and jelly would be needed for 8 sandwiches?
   peanut butter = 16 Tbsp.
   jelly = 24 tsp.

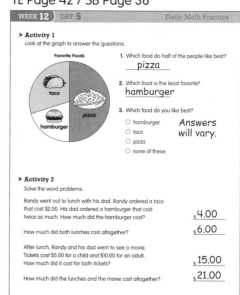

**WEEK 12 DAY 5** — Daily Math Practice

**Activity 1**
Look at the graph to answer the questions.

Favorite Foods

1. Which food do half of the people like best?
   pizza

2. Which food is the least favorite?
   hamburger

3. Which food do you like best?
   ○ hamburger
   ○ taco
   ○ pizza
   ○ none of these
   Answers will vary.

**Activity 2**
Solve the word problems.

Randy went out to lunch with his dad. Randy ordered a taco that cost $2.00. His dad ordered a hamburger that cost twice as much. How much did the hamburger cost?
$ 4.00

How much did both lunches cost altogether?
$ 6.00

After lunch, Randy and his dad went to see a movie. Tickets cost $5.00 for a child and $10.00 for an adult. How much did it cost for both tickets?
$ 15.00

How much did the lunches and the movie cost altogether?
$ 21.00

## TE Page 43 / SB Page 37

**WEEK 13  DAY 1**  Daily Math Practice

1. $58 + 35 + 12 = 105$

2. $\begin{array}{r} 63 \\ -27 \\ \hline ? \end{array}$  ○ 46  ● 36  ○ 30

3. Color the cube.
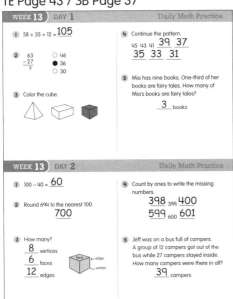

4. Continue the pattern.
45 43 41 **39 37**
**35 33 31**

5. Mia has nine books. One-third of her books are fairy tales. How many of Mia's books are fairy tales?
**3** books

**WEEK 13  DAY 2**  Daily Math Practice

1. $100 - 40 = 60$

2. Round 694 to the nearest 100.
**700**

3. How many?
**8** vertices
**6** faces
**12** edges

4. Count by ones to write the missing numbers.
398 **399** **400**
**599** 600 **601**

5. Jeff was on a bus full of campers. A group of 12 campers got out of the bus while 27 campers stayed inside. How many campers were there in all?
**39** campers

## TE Page 44 / SB Page 38

**WEEK 13  DAY 3**  Daily Math Practice

1. $6 \times \underline{4} = 24$
$24 \div 6 = \underline{4}$

2. $\begin{array}{r} 6 \\ \times 7 \\ \hline 42 \end{array}$   $6)\overline{\phantom{0}7\phantom{0}} \quad \underline{42}$

3. Tyrone bought two cans of paint. The green paint cost $2.57. The white paint cost $4.35. How much did Tyrone spend altogether?
$**6.92**

4.
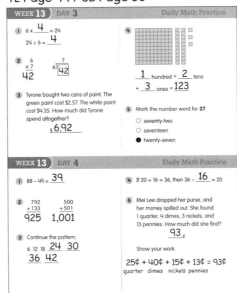
**1** hundred + **2** tens + **3** ones = **123**

5. Mark the number word for **27**.
○ seventy-two
○ seventeen
● twenty-seven

**WEEK 13  DAY 4**  Daily Math Practice

1. $88 - 49 = 39$

2. $\begin{array}{r} 792 \\ +133 \\ \hline 925 \end{array}$   $\begin{array}{r} 500 \\ +501 \\ \hline 1,001 \end{array}$

3. Continue the pattern.
6 12 18 **24 30**
**36 42**

4. If $20 + 16 = 36$, then $36 - \underline{16} = 20$.

5. Mei Lee dropped her purse, and her money spilled out. She found 1 quarter, 4 dimes, 3 nickels, and 13 pennies. How much did she find?
**93**¢

Show your work.
25¢ + 40¢ + 15¢ + 13¢ = 93¢
quarter dimes nickels pennies

## TE Page 45 / SB Page 39

**WEEK 13  DAY 5**  Daily Math Practice

➤ **Activity 1**
Use the chart to answer the questions.

| Bake Sale | | | |
|---|---|---|---|
| tart | cupcake | brownie | cookie |
| 75¢ | 50¢ | 25¢ | 10¢ |

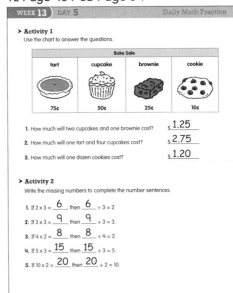

1. How much will two cupcakes and one brownie cost?  $**1.25**
2. How much will one tart and four cupcakes cost?  $**2.75**
3. How much will one dozen cookies cost?  $**1.20**

➤ **Activity 2**
Write the missing numbers to complete the number sentences.

1. If $2 \times 3 = \underline{6}$, then $\underline{6} \div 3 = 2$.
2. If $3 \times 3 = \underline{9}$, then $\underline{9} \div 3 = 3$.
3. If $4 \times 2 = \underline{8}$, then $\underline{8} \div 4 = 2$.
4. If $5 \times 3 = \underline{15}$, then $\underline{15} \div 3 = 5$.
5. If $10 \times 2 = \underline{20}$, then $\underline{20} \div 2 = 10$.

## TE Page 46 / SB Page 40

**WEEK 14  DAY 1**  Daily Math Practice

1. $248 + 354 = 602$

2. $\begin{array}{r} 736 \\ -255 \\ \hline 481 \end{array}$   $\begin{array}{r} 909 \\ -645 \\ \hline 264 \end{array}$

3. Color the trapezoid.
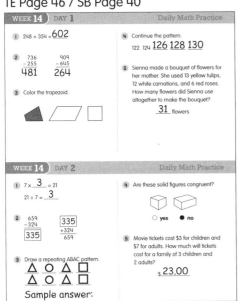

4. Continue the pattern.
122 124 **126 128 130**

5. Sienna made a bouquet of flowers for her mother. She used 13 yellow tulips, 12 white carnations, and 6 red roses. How many flowers did Sienna use altogether to make the bouquet?
**31** flowers

**WEEK 14  DAY 2**  Daily Math Practice

1. $7 \times \underline{3} = 21$
$21 \div 7 = \underline{3}$

2. $\begin{array}{r} 659 \\ -324 \\ \hline 335 \end{array}$   $\begin{array}{r} \boxed{335} \\ +324 \\ \hline 659 \end{array}$

3. Draw a repeating ABAC pattern.
Sample answer:
△ ○ △ □
△ ○ △ □

4. Are these solid figures congruent?
○ yes  ● no

5. Movie tickets cost $3 for children and $7 for adults. How much will tickets cost for a family of 3 children and 2 adults?
$**23.00**

## TE Page 47 / SB Page 41

**WEEK 14  DAY 3**  Daily Math Practice

1. $90 + 40 - 70 = 60$

2. $\begin{array}{r} 5 \\ \times 7 \\ \hline 35 \end{array}$   $\begin{array}{r} 7 \\ \times 5 \\ \hline 35 \end{array}$

3. Circle the butterfly that has a line of symmetry.
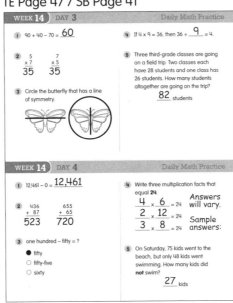

4. If $4 \times 9 = 36$, then $36 \div \underline{9} = 4$.

5. Three third-grade classes are going on a field trip. Two classes each have 28 students and one class has 26 students. How many students altogether are going on the trip?
**82** students

**WEEK 14  DAY 4**  Daily Math Practice

1. $12,461 - 0 = 12,461$

2. $\begin{array}{r} 436 \\ +87 \\ \hline 523 \end{array}$   $\begin{array}{r} 655 \\ +65 \\ \hline 720 \end{array}$

3. one hundred – fifty = ?
● fifty
○ fifty-five
○ sixty

4. Write three multiplication facts that equal 24.
$4 \times 6 = 24$
$2 \times 12 = 24$
$3 \times 8 = 24$
Answers will vary. Sample answers:

5. On Saturday, 75 kids went to the beach, but only 48 kids went swimming. How many kids did **not** swim?
**27** kids

## TE Page 48 / SB Page 42

**WEEK 14  DAY 5**  Daily Math Practice

➤ **Activity 1**
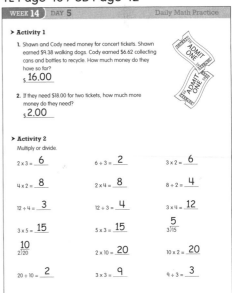

1. Shawn and Cody need money for concert tickets. Shawn earned $9.38 walking dogs. Cody earned $6.62 collecting cans and bottles to recycle. How much money do they have so far?
$**16.00**

2. If they need $18.00 for two tickets, how much more money do they need?
$**2.00**

➤ **Activity 2**
Multiply or divide.

$2 \times 3 = \underline{6}$   $6 \div 3 = \underline{2}$   $3 \times 2 = \underline{6}$
$4 \times 2 = \underline{8}$   $2 \times 4 = \underline{8}$   $8 \div 2 = \underline{4}$
$12 \div 4 = \underline{3}$   $12 \div 3 = \underline{4}$   $3 \times 4 = \underline{12}$
$3 \times 5 = \underline{15}$   $5 \times 3 = \underline{15}$   $3)\overline{15} \quad \underline{5}$
$2)\overline{20} \quad \underline{10}$   $2 \times 10 = \underline{20}$   $10 \times 2 = \underline{20}$
$20 \div 10 = \underline{2}$   $3 \times 3 = \underline{9}$   $9 \div 3 = \underline{3}$

## TE Page 49 / SB Page 43

**WEEK 15  DAY 1**  Daily Math Practice

1. $5 \times \underline{9} = 45$
$45 \div 5 = \underline{9}$

2. $\begin{array}{r} 200 \\ +600 \\ \hline 800 \end{array}$   $\begin{array}{r} 300 \\ +400 \\ \hline 700 \end{array}$

3. Write the missing numbers.
3 hours = **180** minutes
**24** hours = 1 day
**24** months = 2 years

4. Count by threes.
366 369 **372 375 378**
**381 384 387**

5. David has 26 stuffed animals and Tessa has 39. Which operation would you use to find out how many stuffed animals they have altogether?
● addition  ○ multiplication
○ subtraction  ○ division

**WEEK 15  DAY 2**  Daily Math Practice

1. $(18 - 9) \times 4 = \underline{36}$
$9 \times 4 = \underline{36}$

2. $\begin{array}{r} 643 \\ -471 \\ \hline 172 \end{array}$   $\begin{array}{r} 600 \\ -500 \\ \hline 100 \end{array}$

3. Which **two** units could you use to measure juice?
○ centimeters  ● liters
○ ounces  ○ pounds

4. Which amount shows where the decimal point belongs in one dollar and twenty-seven cents?
○ $12.7
○ $.127
● $1.27

5. There are 3 glasses of water in each one-liter bottle. How many liters in all would 9 people need if they each drank 2 glasses of water?
**6** liters

## TE Page 50 / SB Page 44

**WEEK 15  DAY 3**  Daily Math Practice

1. $126 - 120 = 6$

2. $\begin{array}{r} 249 \\ +460 \\ \hline 709 \end{array}$   $\begin{array}{r} \boxed{709} \\ -249 \\ \hline 460 \end{array}$

3. Find the perimeter.
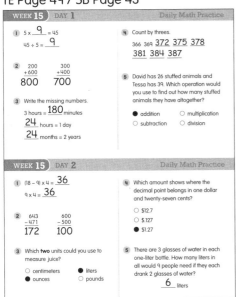
**24** cm

4. If $4 \times 5 = 20$, then $5 \times \underline{4} = 20$.

5. Jasmine baked 2 dozen chocolate chip cookies, 1 dozen oatmeal cookies, and 1 dozen peanut butter cookies for her party. How many cookies did she bake altogether?
● 48  ○ 40  ○ 36

**WEEK 15  DAY 4**  Daily Math Practice

1. $5 \times 6 = \underline{30}$
$6 \times 5 = \underline{30}$

2. two hundred + three hundred = ?
○ four hundred
● five hundred
○ six hundred

3. Mrs. Chang made 137 jars of jam. She sold 93 jars. How many jars does she have left?
**44** jars

4. How many inches are in one foot?
○ 18  ○ 14  ● 12

5. Are these two shapes congruent?
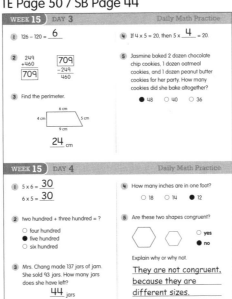
○ yes  ● no

Explain why or why not.
They are not congruent, because they are different sizes.

## TE Page 51 / SB Page 45

**WEEK 15  DAY 5**  Daily Math Practice

➤ **Activity 1**
Make **15** in each direction.
Use these numbers: **1, 2, 3, 5, 6**

| 8 | 3 | 4 |
|---|---|---|
| 1 | 5 | 9 |
| 6 | 7 | 2 |

➤ **Activity 2**
Complete the table.

**Addition Table**

| + | 0 | 1 | 2 | 3 | 4 | 5 | 6 | 7 | 8 | 9 | 10 |
|---|---|---|---|---|---|---|---|---|---|---|---|
| 0 | 0 | 1 | 2 | 3 | 4 | 5 | 6 | 7 | 8 | 9 | 10 |
| 1 | 1 | 2 | 3 | 4 | 5 | 6 | 7 | 8 | 9 | 10 | 11 |
| 2 | 2 | 3 | 4 | 5 | 6 | 7 | 8 | 9 | 10 | 11 | 12 |
| 3 | 3 | 4 | 5 | 6 | 7 | 8 | 9 | 10 | 11 | 12 | 13 |
| 4 | 4 | 5 | 6 | 7 | 8 | 9 | 10 | 11 | 12 | 13 | 14 |
| 5 | 5 | 6 | 7 | 8 | 9 | 10 | 11 | 12 | 13 | 14 | 15 |
| 6 | 6 | 7 | 8 | 9 | 10 | 11 | 12 | 13 | 14 | 15 | 16 |
| 7 | 7 | 8 | 9 | 10 | 11 | 12 | 13 | 14 | 15 | 16 | 17 |
| 8 | 8 | 9 | 10 | 11 | 12 | 13 | 14 | 15 | 16 | 17 | 18 |
| 9 | 9 | 10 | 11 | 12 | 13 | 14 | 15 | 16 | 17 | 18 | 19 |
| 10 | 10 | 11 | 12 | 13 | 14 | 15 | 16 | 17 | 18 | 19 | 20 |

## TE Page 52 / SB Page 46

1. $47 + 40 = 87$
   $47 + 39 = 86$

2. $834 - 617 = 217$    $742 - 328 = 414$

3. Circle the unit used to measure a person's weight.
   cups (pounds) meters grams

4. Round each number to the nearest 10.
   49 is almost 50
   21 is almost 20

5. One ice-cream cone costs 48 cents. Draw Xs on the fewest coins you would use to pay for two ice-cream cones.

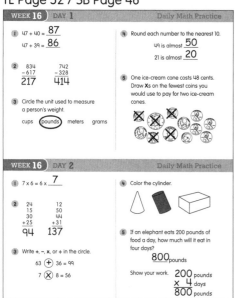

1. $7 \times 6 = 6 \times 7$

2. $24 + 15 + 30 + 25 = 94$    $12 + 50 + 44 + 31 = 137$

3. Write +, −, ×, or ÷ in the circle.
   $63 (+) 36 = 99$
   $7 (\times) 8 = 56$

4. Color the cylinder.

5. If an elephant eats 200 pounds of food a day, how much will it eat in four days?
   800 pounds
   Show your work.
   $200$ pounds
   $\times 4$ days
   $800$ pounds

## TE Page 53 / SB Page 47

1. $25 \div 5 = 5$
   $5 \times 5 = 25$

2. $8 \times 7 = 56$    $7 \times 8 = 56$

3. Write four number sentences using 5, 9, and 45.
   $5 \times 9 = 45$   $45 \div 5 = 9$
   $9 \times 5 = 45$   $45 \div 9 = 5$

4. Circle the best estimate.
   $89 + 67 = ?$
   (160) 150 170

5. Mr. Tanaka makes birdhouses. He made 36 blue ones, 24 brown ones, and 16 green ones. How many birdhouses did he make in all?
   76 birdhouses

1. $124 - 24 = 100$

2. $384 + 169 = 553$    $426 + 491 = 917$

3. Write the numbers below in order from smallest to largest.
   29  191  48  196  9
   9  29  48  191  196

4. Round each number to the nearest 10.
   27 is almost 30
   62 is almost 60
   118 is almost 120

5. A bag of peanuts cost Bonnie 65¢. She gave the clerk three quarters. How much change did Bonnie get back?
   10 ¢

## TE Page 54 / SB Page 48

**Activity 1**
Look at each Input and Output number. Figure out the pattern and complete the chart.
What is the rule for the pattern?
The input number x2 equals the output number.

| Input | Output |
|---|---|
| 4 | 8 |
| 9 | 18 |
| 12 | 24 |
| 15 | 30 |
| 20 | 40 |
| 100 | 200 |

**Activity 2**
Round to the nearest 10.

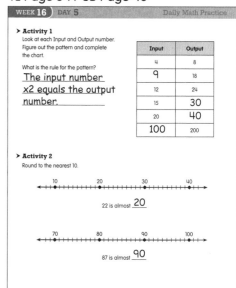

22 is almost 20

87 is almost 90

## TE Page 55 / SB Page 49

1. $120 - 56 = 64$

2. $270 + 158 = 428$    $490 + 204 = 694$

3. Circle the number two hundred sixty-six.
   2,066 (266) 626

4. Circle the odd number.
   72 (63) 92

5. Madison eats 3 pieces of fruit every day. How many days will it take Madison to eat 18 pieces?
   6 days
   Show your work.
   $3\overline{)18}$ 6 days  pieces of fruit

1. $90 - 63 = 27$

2. $3 \times 8 = 24$   $4 \times 8 = 32$   $5 \times 8 = 40$

3. Look at the clock. Circle the time that is a half hour later.

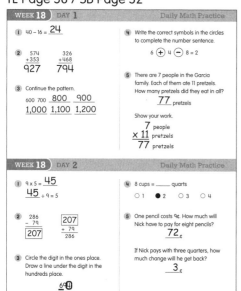
6:30
(6:40)
6:50

4. If $32 + 6 = 38$, then $38 - 6 = 32$.

5. Arturo has 25 toy dinosaurs. His brother gave him 6 more. How many toy dinosaurs does Arturo have now?
   31 toy dinosaurs
   Show your work.
   $25$ toy dinosaurs
   $+ 6$ more
   $31$ toy dinosaurs

## TE Page 56 / SB Page 50

1. $2 \times 9 = 18$
   $9 \times 2 = 18$

2. $153 - 27 = 126$    $932 - 271 = 661$

3. Write the expanded number.
   $78 = 70 + 8$
   $92 = 90 + 2$
   $133 = 100 + 30 + 3$

4. Write the correct symbol in the circle.
   < = >
   $647 (<) 796$
   $895 (>) 598$

5. One week has seven days. How many days are in seven weeks?
   49 days

1. $32 \div 8 = 4$
   $8 \times 4 = 32$

2. $9 \times 6 = 54$   $9 \times 7 = 63$   $9 \times 8 = 72$

3. Color the cone.

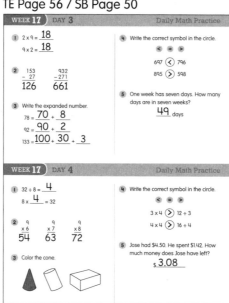

4. Write the correct symbol in the circle.
   < = >
   $3 \times 4 (>) 12 \div 3$
   $4 \times 4 (>) 16 \div 4$

5. Jose had $4.50. He spent $1.42. How much money does Jose have left?
   $ 3.08

## TE Page 57 / SB Page 51

**Activity 1**
Look at the schedule to answer the questions.

**Sofia's Schedule**

| | |
|---|---|
| 6:00 a.m. Wake up | 12:00 p.m. Lunch |
| 8:00 a.m. School starts | 3:00 p.m. School ends |
| 10:30 a.m. Recess | 5:00 p.m. Do homework |

1. What does Sofia do at 12:00 p.m.?   eats lunch
2. At what time does Sofia wake up?   6:00 a.m.
3. How long is Sofia at school?   7 hours

**Activity 2**
Complete the table.

**Multiplication Table**

| x | 1 | 2 | 3 | 4 | 5 | 6 | 7 | 8 | 9 | 10 |
|---|---|---|---|---|---|---|---|---|---|---|
| 1 | 1 | 2 | 3 | 4 | 5 | 6 | 7 | 8 | 9 | 10 |
| 2 | 2 | 4 | 6 | 8 | 10 | 12 | 14 | 16 | 18 | 20 |
| 3 | 3 | 6 | 9 | 12 | 15 | 18 | 21 | 24 | 27 | 30 |
| 4 | 4 | 8 | 12 | 16 | 20 | 24 | 28 | 32 | 36 | 40 |
| 5 | 5 | 10 | 15 | 20 | 25 | 30 | 35 | 40 | 45 | 50 |
| 6 | 6 | 12 | 18 | 24 | 30 | 36 | 42 | 48 | 54 | 60 |
| 7 | 7 | 14 | 21 | 28 | 35 | 42 | 49 | 56 | 63 | 70 |
| 8 | 8 | 16 | 24 | 32 | 40 | 48 | 56 | 64 | 72 | 80 |
| 9 | 9 | 18 | 27 | 36 | 45 | 54 | 63 | 72 | 81 | 90 |
| 10 | 10 | 20 | 30 | 40 | 50 | 60 | 70 | 80 | 90 | 100 |

## TE Page 58 / SB Page 52

1. $40 - 16 = 24$

2. $574 + 353 = 927$    $326 + 468 = 794$

3. Continue the pattern.
   600 700 800 900
   1,000 1,100 1,200

4. Write the correct symbols in the circles to complete the number sentence.
   $6 (+) 4 (-) 8 = 2$

5. There are 7 people in the Garcia family. Each of them ate 11 pretzels. How many pretzels did they eat in all?
   77 pretzels
   Show your work.
   $7$ people
   $\times 11$ pretzels
   $77$ pretzels

1. $9 \times 5 = 45$
   $45 \div 9 = 5$

2. $286 - 79 = 207$    $207 + 79 = 286$

3. Circle the digit in the ones place. Draw a line under the digit in the hundreds place.
   6(9)0̲

4. 8 cups = ___ quarts
   ○ 1   ● 2   ○ 3   ○ 4

5. One pencil costs 9¢. How much will Nick have to pay for eight pencils?
   72 ¢
   If Nick pays with three quarters, how much change will he get back?
   3 ¢

## TE Page 59 / SB Page 53

1. $4 \times 8 = 32$
   $8 \times 4 = 32$

2. $385 + 74 = 459$    $459 - 385 = 74$

3. What fraction is shaded?

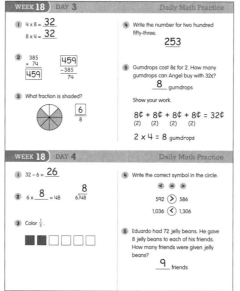
$\frac{6}{8}$

4. Write the number for two hundred fifty-three.
   253

5. Gumdrops cost 8¢ for 2. How many gumdrops can Angel buy with 32¢?
   8 gumdrops
   Show your work.
   8¢ + 8¢ + 8¢ + 8¢ = 32¢
   (2) (2) (2) (2)
   $2 \times 4 = 8$ gumdrops

1. $32 - 6 = 26$

2. $6 \times 8 = 48$    $6\overline{)48} = 8$

3. Color $\frac{1}{3}$.

4. Write the correct symbol in the circle.
   < = >
   $592 (>) 586$
   $1,036 (<) 1,306$

5. Eduardo had 72 jelly beans. He gave 8 jelly beans to each of his friends. How many friends were given jelly beans?
   9 friends

## TE Page 60 / SB Page 54

**Activity 1**
Alicia has five dogs. She wants to give three bones to each of them. How many bones will Alicia need?

1. Use pictures to solve the problem.

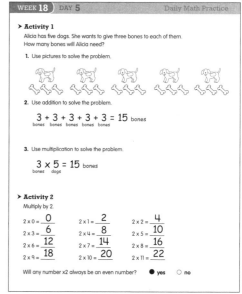

2. Use addition to solve the problem.
   $3 + 3 + 3 + 3 + 3 = 15$ bones
   bones bones bones bones bones

3. Use multiplication to solve the problem.
   $3 \times 5 = 15$ bones
   bones dogs

**Activity 2**
Multiply by 2.
$2 \times 0 = 0$    $2 \times 1 = 2$    $2 \times 2 = 4$
$2 \times 3 = 6$    $2 \times 4 = 8$    $2 \times 5 = 10$
$2 \times 6 = 12$    $2 \times 7 = 14$    $2 \times 8 = 16$
$2 \times 9 = 18$    $2 \times 10 = 20$    $2 \times 11 = 22$

Will any number x2 always be an even number?   ● yes   ○ no

## TE Page 61 / SB Page 55

**WEEK 19 · DAY 1 — Daily Math Practice**

1. 75 + 22 = **97**
   95 + 22 = **117**

2. 384 − 106 = **278**      1,000 − 500 = **500**

3. 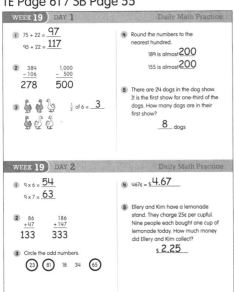 ½ of 6 = **3**

4. Round the numbers to the nearest hundred.
   189 is almost **200**
   155 is almost **200**

5. There are 24 dogs in the dog show. It is the first show for one-third of the dogs. How many dogs are in their first show?
   **8** dogs

**WEEK 19 · DAY 2 — Daily Math Practice**

1. 9 × 6 = **54**
   9 × 7 = **63**

2. 86 + 47 = **133**      186 + 147 = **333**

3. Circle the odd numbers.
   (23) (81) 18 34 (65)

4. 467¢ = $ **4.67**

5. Ellery and Kim have a lemonade stand. They charge 25¢ per cupful. Nine people each bought one cup of lemonade today. How much money did Ellery and Kim collect?
   $ **2.25**

## TE Page 62 / SB Page 56

**WEEK 19 · DAY 3 — Daily Math Practice**

1. 104 − 14 = **90**

2. **9** × 4 = 36      4)36 → **9**

3. Find the perimeter.
   **26** feet

4. 4 tens and 9 ones = **49**
   7 tens and 6 ones = **76**

5. Write number sentences using 7, 3, and 21.
   **3** × **7** = 21
   **7** × **3** = 21
   **21** ÷ **3** = 7
   **21** ÷ **7** = 3

**WEEK 19 · DAY 4 — Daily Math Practice**

1. **5** × 9 = 45
   45 ÷ 9 = **5**

2. 32 + 46 = **106**      30 30 + 50 = **110**

3. How many 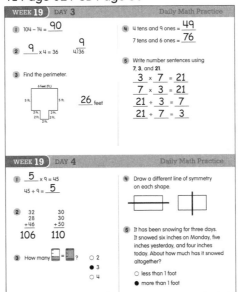 = ?   ○ 2  ● 3  ○ 4

4. Draw a different line of symmetry on each shape.

5. It has been snowing for three days. It snowed six inches on Monday, five inches yesterday, and four inches today. About how much has it snowed altogether?
   ○ less than 1 foot
   ● more than 1 foot

## TE Page 63 / SB Page 57

**WEEK 19 · DAY 5 — Daily Math Practice**

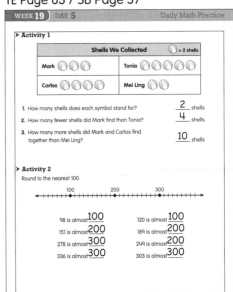

▶ Activity 1

| Shells We Collected | (○ = 2 shells) |
|---|---|
| Mark ○○○ | Tonia ○○○○○ |
| Carlos ○○○ | Mei Ling ○○ |

1. How many shells does each symbol stand for? **2** shells
2. How many fewer shells did Mark find than Tonia? **4** shells
3. How many more shells did Mark and Carlos find together than Mei Ling? **10** shells

▶ Activity 2
Round to the nearest 100.

98 is almost **100**      120 is almost **100**
151 is almost **200**     189 is almost **200**
278 is almost **300**     249 is almost **200**
336 is almost **300**     303 is almost **300**

## TE Page 64 / SB Page 58

**WEEK 20 · DAY 1 — Daily Math Practice**

1. 5 × 8 = **40**
   6 × 8 = **48**

2. 819 − 726 = **93**      927 − 534 = **393**

3. Color ⅘.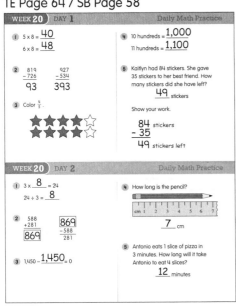

4. 10 hundreds = **1,000**
   11 hundreds = **1,100**

5. Kaitlyn had 84 stickers. She gave 35 stickers to her best friend. How many stickers did she have left?
   **49** stickers
   Show your work.
   84 − 35 = **49** stickers left

**WEEK 20 · DAY 2 — Daily Math Practice**

1. 3 × **8** = 24
   24 ÷ 3 = **8**

2. 588 + 281 = **869**      **869** − 588 = **281**

3. 1,450 − **1,450** = 0

4. How long is the pencil?
   **7** cm

5. Antonio eats 1 slice of pizza in 3 minutes. How long will it take Antonio to eat 4 slices?
   **12** minutes

## TE Page 65 / SB Page 59

**WEEK 20 · DAY 3 — Daily Math Practice**

1. 550 − 241 = **309**

2. 5 × **10** = 50      5)50 → **10**

3. Color ¼.
   ♥♥♡♡♡♡♡♡
   ¼ of 8 = **2**

4. What is the distance from **a** to **b** called?
   ○ line
   ○ angle
   ● line segment

5. Maya made 36 rag dolls to sell. She sold half of the dolls. How many dolls does she have left?
   **18** dolls

**WEEK 20 · DAY 4 — Daily Math Practice**

1. 6 × 7 = 7 × **6**

2. $3.55 + 1.29 = **$4.84**      $4.22 − 2.13 = **$2.09**

3. Divide the octagon into fourths. Color ¾.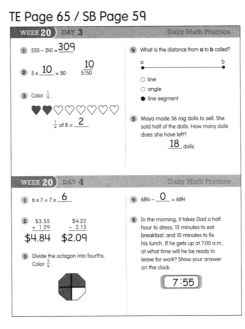

4. 684 − **0** = 684

5. In the morning, it takes Dad a half hour to dress, 15 minutes to eat breakfast, and 10 minutes to fix his lunch. If he gets up at 7:00 a.m., at what time will he be ready to leave for work? Show your answer on the clock.
   **7:55**

## TE Page 66 / SB Page 60

**WEEK 20 · DAY 5 — Daily Math Practice**

| Ice-Cream Sundae | |
|---|---|
| ice cream .......... 60¢ per scoop | whipped cream .......... 24¢ |
| banana .......... 10¢ per slice | walnuts .......... 18¢ |
| chocolate sauce .......... 15¢ | cherry .......... 20¢ |

1. Read the sign. How much does this sundae cost?
   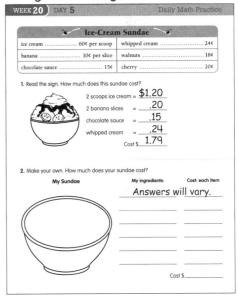
   2 scoops ice cream = **$1.20**
   2 banana slices = **.20**
   chocolate sauce = **.15**
   whipped cream = **.24**
   Cost $ **1.79**

2. Make your own. How much does your sundae cost?
   My Sundae      My ingredients:      Cost: each item
   **Answers will vary.**
   Cost $

## TE Page 67 / SB Page 61

**WEEK 21 · DAY 1 — Daily Math Practice**

1. 9 × **2** = 18
   18 ÷ 9 = **2**

2. 845 − 36 = **809**      **809** + 36 = **845**

3. Circle the best estimate.
   196 − 54 = ?
   ○ 100   ● 150   ○ 200

4. Count by thousands.
   1,000 2,000 **3,000 4,000 5,000 6,000 7,000**

5. Andrew had 24¢. Then his mom gave him a quarter and his dad gave him 43¢. How much money does he have now?
   **92** ¢

**WEEK 21 · DAY 2 — Daily Math Practice**

1. 8 × 9 = **72**
   **72** ÷ 8 = 9

2. 9,463 + 1,025 = **10,488**

3. Write a word problem for 3 × 4 = 12.
   **Three friends each have four cookies. How many cookies do they have in all?**
   Sample answer:

4. Expand the numbers.
   683 = **600** + **80** + **3**
   809 = **800** + **9**

5. Terri has three kinds of cats. The Siamese weighs 4.5 kilograms (kg), the tabby weighs 3.6 kilograms, and the Persian weighs 2.3 kilograms. How much do the cats weigh altogether?
   **10.4** kg

## TE Page 68 / SB Page 62

**WEEK 21 · DAY 3 — Daily Math Practice**

1. 1,005 + 2,025 = **3,030**

2. 654 − 364 = **290**      893 − 422 = **471**

3. What is the name of this solid figure?
   ○ cone
   ○ sphere
   ● cylinder

4. Write an even number that is greater than 10 and less than 20.
   **12**
   OR 14, 16, 18

5. One box of popcorn costs $0.65. How much will three boxes cost?
   $ **1.95**
   Show your work:
   $0.65 × 3 = **$1.95**

**WEEK 21 · DAY 4 — Daily Math Practice**

1. 9 × 8 = **72**
   9 × 9 = **81**

2. 4 × **8** = 32      4)32 → **8**

3. 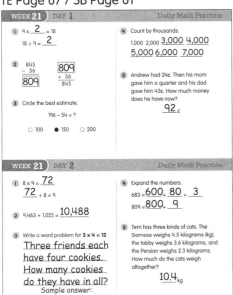 = $ **2.46**

4. 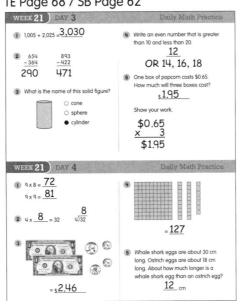 = **127**

5. Whale shark eggs are about 30 cm long. Ostrich eggs are about 18 cm long. About how much longer is a whale shark egg than an ostrich egg?
   **12** cm

## TE Page 69 / SB Page 63

**WEEK 21 · DAY 5 — Daily Math Practice**

Use the graph to answer the questions.

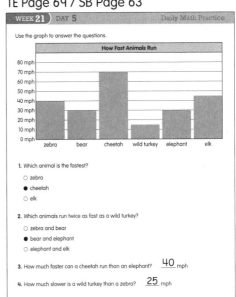

How Fast Animals Run (zebra, bear, cheetah, wild turkey, elephant, elk)

1. Which animal is the fastest?
   ○ zebra
   ● cheetah
   ○ elk

2. Which animals run twice as fast as a wild turkey?
   ○ zebra and bear
   ● bear and elephant
   ○ elephant and elk

3. How much faster can a cheetah run than an elephant? **40** mph

4. How much slower is a wild turkey than a zebra? **25** mph

## TE Page 70 / SB Page 64

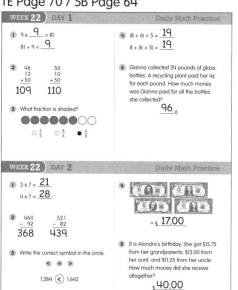

**WEEK 22 DAY 1** — Daily Math Practice

1. $9 \times \underline{9} = 81$
   $81 \div 9 = \underline{9}$

2. $46 + 13 + 50 = 109$
   $50 + 10 + 50 = 110$

3. What fraction is shaded?
   ○ $\frac{2}{3}$  ○ $\frac{8}{6}$  ● $\frac{6}{8}$

4. $(8 + 6) + 5 = \underline{19}$
   $8 + (6 + 5) = \underline{19}$

5. Gianna collected 24 pounds of glass bottles. A recycling plant paid her 4¢ for each pound. How much money was Gianna paid for all the bottles she collected?
   $\underline{96}$ ¢

**WEEK 22 DAY 2** — Daily Math Practice

1. $3 \times 7 = \underline{21}$
   $4 \times 7 = \underline{28}$

2. $460 - 92 = 368$
   $521 - 82 = 439$

3. Write the correct symbol in the circle.
   <  =  >
   $1,264 \; \boxed{<} \; 1,642$

4. = $ \underline{17.00}$

5. It is Alondra's birthday. She got $15.75 from her grandparents, $13.00 from her aunt, and $11.25 from her uncle. How much money did she receive altogether?
   $ \underline{40.00}$

## TE Page 71 / SB Page 65

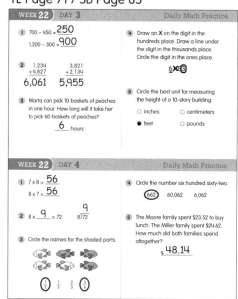

**WEEK 22 DAY 3** — Daily Math Practice

1. $700 - 450 = \underline{250}$
   $1,200 - 300 = \underline{900}$

2. $1,234 + 4,827 = 6,061$
   $3,821 + 2,134 = 5,955$

3. Marta can pick 10 baskets of peaches in one hour. How long will it take her to pick 60 baskets of peaches?
   $\underline{6}$ hours

4. Draw an **X** on the digit in the hundreds place. Draw a line under the digit in the thousands place. Circle the digit in the ones place.
   6 X 3 circled 9

5. Circle the best unit for measuring the height of a 10-story building.
   ○ inches   ○ centimeters
   ● feet     ○ pounds

**WEEK 22 DAY 4** — Daily Math Practice

1. $7 \times 8 = \underline{56}$
   $8 \times 7 = \underline{56}$

2. $8 \times \underline{9} = 72$   $8\overline{)72}$ = 9

3. Circle the names for the shaded parts.
   $\frac{1}{3}$   $\frac{1}{3}$   $\frac{2}{3}$   $\frac{2}{3}$

4. Circle the number six hundred sixty-two.
   (662)  60,062  6,062

5. The Moore family spent $23.52 to buy lunch. The Miller family spent $24.62. How much did both families spend altogether?
   $ \underline{48.14}$

## TE Page 72 / SB Page 66

**WEEK 22 DAY 5** — Daily Math Practice

> **Activity 1**

A factory makes bicycles every day. The colors of the bicycles are black, red, blue, green, and purple. Red bikes are the favorite of most children. How many days would it take the factory to make 500 bicycles?

Which sentence is needed to answer the question?
○ More boys than girls ride bikes.
○ The factory is open 10 hours a day.
● The factory can make 100 bikes each day.

Now answer the question.
$\underline{5}$ days

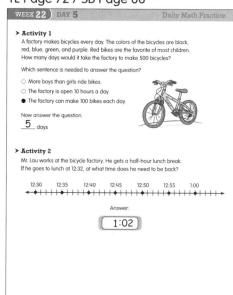

> **Activity 2**

Mr. Lau works at the bicycle factory. He gets a half-hour lunch break. If he goes to lunch at 12:32, at what time does he need to be back?

12:30  12:35  12:40  12:45  12:50  12:55  1:00

Answer:
$\boxed{1:02}$

## TE Page 73 / SB Page 67

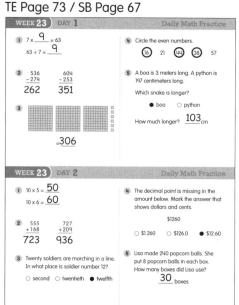

**WEEK 23 DAY 1** — Daily Math Practice

1. $7 \times \underline{9} = 63$
   $63 \div 7 = \underline{9}$

2. $536 - 274 = 262$
   $604 - 253 = 351$

3. = $\underline{306}$

4. Circle the even numbers.
   (16)  21  (44)  (38)  57

5. A boa is 3 meters long. A python is 197 centimeters long.
   Which snake is longer?
   ● boa   ○ python
   How much longer? $\underline{103}$ cm

**WEEK 23 DAY 2** — Daily Math Practice

1. $10 \times 5 = \underline{50}$
   $10 \times 6 = \underline{60}$

2. $555 + 168 = 723$
   $727 + 209 = 936$

3. Twenty soldiers are marching in a line. In what place is soldier number 12?
   ○ second  ○ twentieth  ● twelfth

4. The decimal point is missing in the amount below. Mark the answer that shows dollars and cents.
   $1260
   ○ $1.260  ○ $126.0  ● $12.60

5. Lisa made 240 popcorn balls. She put 8 popcorn balls in each box. How many boxes did Lisa use?
   $\underline{30}$ boxes

## TE Page 74 / SB Page 68

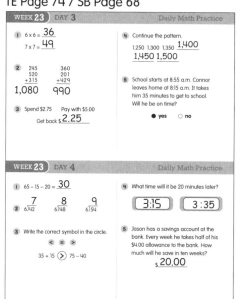

**WEEK 23 DAY 3** — Daily Math Practice

1. $6 \times 6 = \underline{36}$
   $7 \times 7 = \underline{49}$

2. $245 + 520 + 315 = 1,080$
   $360 + 201 + 429 = 990$

3. Spend $2.75  Pay with $5.00
   Get back $ \underline{2.25}$

4. Continue the pattern.
   1,250  1,300  1,350  $\underline{1,400}$
   $\underline{1,450}$  $\underline{1,500}$

5. School starts at 8:55 a.m. Connor leaves home at 8:15 a.m. It takes him 35 minutes to get to school. Will he be on time?
   ● yes   ○ no

**WEEK 23 DAY 4** — Daily Math Practice

1. $65 - 15 - 20 = \underline{30}$

2. $6\overline{)42} = 7$   $6\overline{)48} = 8$   $6\overline{)54} = 9$

3. Write the correct symbol in the circle.
   <  =  >
   $35 + 15 \; \boxed{>} \; 75 - 40$

4. What time will it be 20 minutes later?
   $\boxed{3:15}$   $\boxed{3:35}$

5. Jason has a savings account at the bank. Every week he takes half of his $4.00 allowance to the bank. How much will he save in ten weeks?
   $ \underline{20.00}$

## TE Page 75 / SB Page 69

**WEEK 23 DAY 5** — Daily Math Practice

> **Activity 1**

1. Hot dogs come in packages of 10. Complete the function table.

| Number of Packages | 1 | 2 | 3 | 4 | 5 | 6 | 7 | 8 |
|---|---|---|---|---|---|---|---|---|
| Number of Hot Dogs | 10 | 20 | 30 | 40 | 50 | 60 | 70 | 80 |

2. Circle the operations you can use.
   (addition)  subtraction  (multiplication)  division

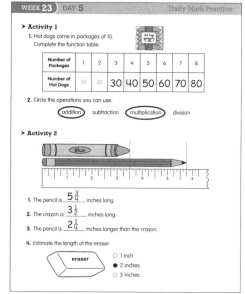

> **Activity 2**

1. The pencil is $5\frac{3}{4}$ inches long.
2. The crayon is $3\frac{1}{2}$ inches long.
3. The pencil is $2\frac{1}{4}$ inches longer than the crayon.
4. Estimate the length of the eraser.
   eraser
   ○ 1 inch
   ● 2 inches
   ○ 3 inches

## TE Page 76 / SB Page 70

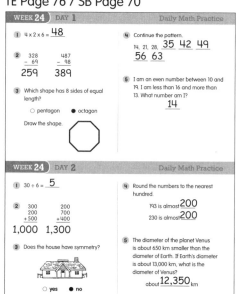

**WEEK 24 DAY 1** — Daily Math Practice

1. $4 \times 2 \times 6 = \underline{48}$

2. $328 - 69 = 259$
   $487 - 98 = 389$

3. Which shape has 8 sides of equal length?
   ○ pentagon  ● octagon
   Draw the shape.

4. Continue the pattern.
   14, 21, 28, $\underline{35}$ $\underline{42}$ $\underline{49}$
   $\underline{56}$ $\underline{63}$

5. I am an even number between 10 and 19. I am less than 16 and more than 13. What number am I?
   $\underline{14}$

**WEEK 24 DAY 2** — Daily Math Practice

1. $30 \div 6 = \underline{5}$

2. $300 + 500 = 800$ ... $1,000$
   $200 + 700 + 400 = 1,300$

3. Does the house have symmetry?
   ○ yes  ● no

4. Round the numbers to the nearest hundred.
   193 is almost $\underline{200}$
   230 is almost $\underline{200}$

5. The diameter of the planet Venus is about 650 km smaller than the diameter of Earth. If Earth's diameter is about 13,000 km, what is the diameter of Venus?
   about $\underline{12,350}$ km

## TE Page 77 / SB Page 71

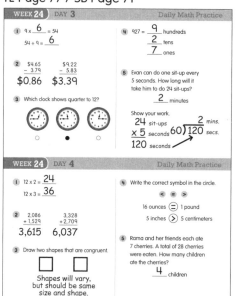

**WEEK 24 DAY 3** — Daily Math Practice

1. $9 \times \underline{6} = 54$
   $54 \div 9 = \underline{6}$

2. $$4.65 - 3.79 = $0.86$
   $$9.22 - 5.83 = $3.39$

3. Which clock shows quarter to 12?
   ○  ●  ○

4. $927 = \underline{9}$ hundreds
   $\underline{2}$ tens
   $\underline{7}$ ones

5. Evan can do one sit-up every 5 seconds. How long will it take him to do 24 sit-ups?
   $\underline{2}$ minutes
   Show your work.
   24 sit-ups
   × 5 seconds
   120 seconds
   $60\overline{)120}$ = 2 mins.  120 secs.

**WEEK 24 DAY 4** — Daily Math Practice

1. $12 \times 2 = \underline{24}$
   $12 \times 3 = \underline{36}$

2. $2,086 + 1,529 = 3,615$
   $3,328 + 2,709 = 6,037$

3. Draw two shapes that are congruent.
   Shapes will vary, but should be same size and shape.

4. Write the correct symbol in the circle.
   <  =  >
   16 ounces $\boxed{=}$ 1 pound
   5 inches $\boxed{>}$ 5 centimeters

5. Rama and her friends each ate 7 cherries. A total of 28 cherries were eaten. How many children ate the cherries?
   $\underline{4}$ children

## TE Page 78 / SB Page 72

**WEEK 24 DAY 5** — Daily Math Practice

> **Activity 1**

Complete the table.
How many treats will each person get?          ☺ = 1 person

| | | |
|---|---|---|
| There are 25 pretzels | ☺☺☺☺☺ | $\underline{5}$ pretzels each |
| There are 24 jelly beans | ☺☺☺☺ | $\underline{6}$ jelly beans each |
| There are 18 cookies | ☺☺☺ | $\underline{6}$ cookies each |
| There are 16 peanuts | ☺☺ | $\underline{8}$ peanuts each |

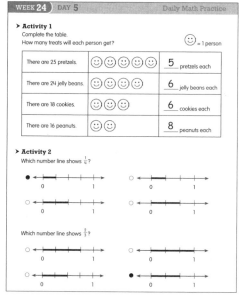

> **Activity 2**

Which number line shows $\frac{1}{4}$?
(● left top) 0 ——— 1     ○ 0 ——— 1
○ 0 ——— 1                  ○ 0 ——— 1

Which number line shows $\frac{2}{3}$?
○ 0 ——— 1                  ○ 0 ——— 1
○ 0 ——— 1                  ● 0 ——— 1

Daily Math Practice • EMC 752 • © Evan-Moor Corp.

## TE Page 79 / SB Page 73

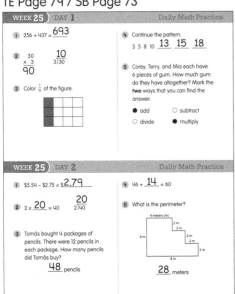

**WEEK 25 · DAY 1** — Daily Math Practice

1. 256 + 437 = __693__

2. 30
   × 3
   __90__        __10__
                3)30

3. Color ⅓ of the figure.

4. Continue the pattern.
   3 5 8 10 __13__ __15__ __18__

5. Corey, Terry, and Mia each have 6 pieces of gum. How much gum do they have altogether? Mark the **two** ways that you can find the answer.
   ● add        ○ subtract
   ○ divide     ● multiply

**WEEK 25 · DAY 2** — Daily Math Practice

1. $5.54 − $2.75 = $__2.79__

2. 2 × __20__ = 40        __20__
                        2)40

3. Tomás bought 4 packages of pencils. There were 12 pencils in each package. How many pencils did Tomás buy?
   __48__ pencils

4. 46 + __14__ = 60

5. What is the perimeter?
   4 meters (m)
   __28__ meters

## TE Page 80 / SB Page 74

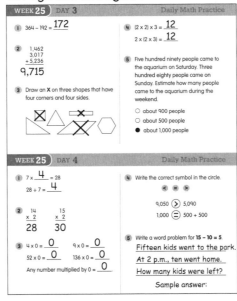

**WEEK 25 · DAY 3** — Daily Math Practice

1. 364 − 192 = __172__

2. 1,462
   3,017
   + 5,236
   __9,715__

3. Draw an X on three shapes that have four corners and four sides.

4. (2 × 2) × 3 = __12__
   2 × (2 × 3) = __12__

5. Five hundred ninety people came to the aquarium on Saturday. Three hundred eighty people came on Sunday. Estimate how many people came to the aquarium during the weekend.
   ○ about 900 people
   ○ about 500 people
   ● about 1,000 people

**WEEK 25 · DAY 4** — Daily Math Practice

1. 7 × __4__ = 28
   28 ÷ 7 = __4__

2. 14       15
   × 2      × 2
   __28__   __30__

3. 4 × 0 = __0__        9 × 0 = __0__
   52 × 0 = __0__      136 × 0 = __0__
   Any number multiplied by 0 = __0__

4. Write the correct symbol in the circle.
   < = >
   9,050 (>) 5,090
   1,000 (=) 500 + 500

5. Write a word problem for **15 − 10 = 5**.
   Sample answer:
   __Fifteen kids went to the park.__
   __At 2 p.m., ten went home.__
   __How many kids were left?__

## TE Page 81 / SB Page 75

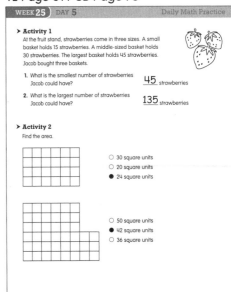

**WEEK 25 · DAY 5** — Daily Math Practice

> **Activity 1**
At the fruit stand, strawberries come in three sizes. A small basket holds 15 strawberries. A middle-sized basket holds 30 strawberries. The largest basket holds 45 strawberries. Jacob bought three baskets.

1. What is the smallest number of strawberries Jacob could have?    __45__ strawberries

2. What is the largest number of strawberries Jacob could have?    __135__ strawberries

> **Activity 2**
Find the area.

   ○ 30 square units
   ○ 20 square units
   ● 24 square units

   ○ 50 square units
   ● 42 square units
   ○ 36 square units

## TE Page 82 / SB Page 76

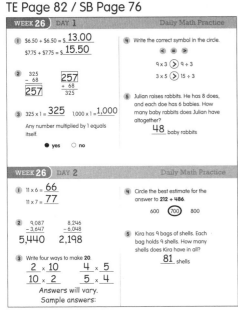

**WEEK 26 · DAY 1** — Daily Math Practice

1. $6.50 + $6.50 = $__13.00__
   $7.75 + $7.75 = $__15.50__

2. 325
   − 68       __257__
   __257__    + 68
              325

3. 325 × 1 = __325__    1,000 × 1 = __1,000__
   Any number multiplied by 1 equals itself.
   ● yes    ○ no

4. Write the correct symbol in the circle.
   < = >
   9 × 3 (>) 9 ÷ 3
   3 × 5 (>) 15 ÷ 3

5. Julian raises rabbits. He has 8 does, and each doe has 6 babies. How many baby rabbits does Julian have altogether?
   __48__ baby rabbits

**WEEK 26 · DAY 2** — Daily Math Practice

1. 11 × 6 = __66__
   11 × 7 = __77__

2. 9,087       8,246
   − 3,647     − 6,048
   __5,440__   __2,198__

3. Write four ways to make **20**.
   __2__ × __10__    __4__ × __5__
   __10__ × __2__    __5__ × __4__
   Answers will vary.
   Sample answers:

4. Circle the best estimate for the answer to **212 + 486**.
   600   (700)   800

5. Kira has 9 bags of shells. Each bag holds 9 shells. How many shells does Kira have in all?
   __81__ shells

## TE Page 83 / SB Page 77

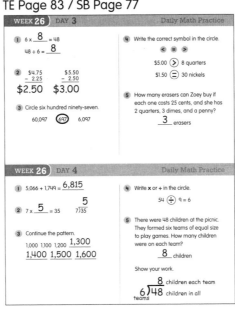

**WEEK 26 · DAY 3** — Daily Math Practice

1. 6 × __8__ = 48
   48 ÷ 6 = __8__

2. $4.75       $5.50
   − 2.25      − 2.50
   __$2.50__   __$3.00__

3. Circle six hundred ninety-seven.
   60,097   (697)   6,097

4. Write the correct symbol in the circle.
   < = >
   $5.00 (>) 8 quarters
   $1.50 (=) 30 nickels

5. How many erasers can Zoey buy if each one costs 25 cents, and she has 2 quarters, 3 dimes, and a penny?
   __3__ erasers

**WEEK 26 · DAY 4** — Daily Math Practice

1. 5,066 + 1,749 = __6,815__

2. 7 × __5__ = 35        __5__
                        7)35

3. Continue the pattern.
   1,000 1,100 1,200 __1,300__
   __1,400__ __1,500__ __1,600__

4. Write × or ÷ in the circle.
   54 (÷) 9 = 6

5. There were 48 children at the picnic. They formed six teams of equal size to play games. How many children were on each team?
   __8__ children
   Show your work.
              8 children each team
   6)48     children in all
   teams

## TE Page 84 / SB Page 78

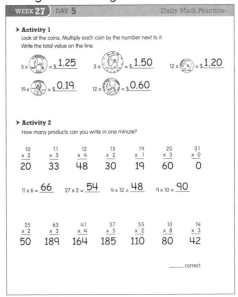

**WEEK 26 · DAY 5** — Daily Math Practice

> **Activity 1**
Aunt Emily planted 6 rows of 9 daisies and 8 rows of 7 tulips in her garden this year. Last year she planted 100 flowers. Did she plant more or less flowers this year?
   ● more    ○ less
   How many more or less?    __10__ flowers

> **Activity 2**
A quadrilateral is a plane shape with four sides and four angles. Color all the shapes that are quadrilaterals.

## TE Page 85 / SB Page 79

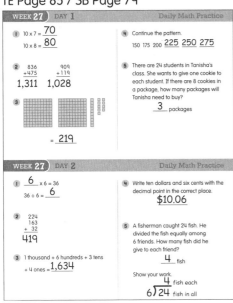

**WEEK 27 · DAY 1** — Daily Math Practice

1. 10 × 7 = __70__
   10 × 8 = __80__

2. 836       909
   + 475     + 119
   __1,311__ __1,028__

3. = __219__

4. Continue the pattern.
   150 175 200 __225__ __250__ __275__

5. There are 24 students in Tanisha's class. She wants to give one cookie to each student. If there are 8 cookies in a package, how many packages will Tanisha need to buy?
   __3__ packages

**WEEK 27 · DAY 2** — Daily Math Practice

1. __6__ × 6 = 36
   36 ÷ 6 = __6__

2. 224
   163
   + 32
   __419__

3. 1 thousand + 6 hundreds + 3 tens + 4 ones = __1,634__

4. Write ten dollars and six cents with the decimal point in the correct place.
   __$10.06__

5. A fisherman caught 24 fish. He divided the fish equally among 6 friends. How many fish did he give to each friend?
   __4__ fish
   Show your work.
            4 fish each
   6)24     fish in all

## TE Page 86 / SB Page 80

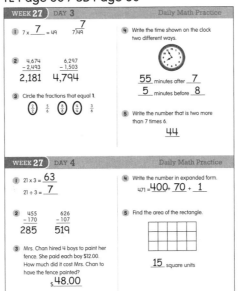

**WEEK 27 · DAY 3** — Daily Math Practice

1. 7 × __7__ = 49        __7__
                        7)49

2. 4,674       6,297
   − 2,493     − 1,503
   __2,181__   __4,794__

3. Circle the fractions that equal **1**.
   (6/6)   0   (3/3)

4. Write the time shown on the clock two different ways.
   __55__ minutes after __7__
   __5__ minutes before __8__

5. Write the number that is two more than 7 times 6.
   __44__

**WEEK 27 · DAY 4** — Daily Math Practice

1. 21 × 3 = __63__
   21 ÷ 3 = __7__

2. 455       626
   − 170     − 107
   __285__   __519__

3. Mrs. Chan hired 4 boys to paint her fence. She paid each boy $12.00. How much did it cost Mrs. Chan to have the fence painted?
   $__48.00__

4. Write the number in expanded form.
   471 = __400__ + __70__ + __1__

5. Find the area of the rectangle.
   __15__ square units

## TE Page 87 / SB Page 81

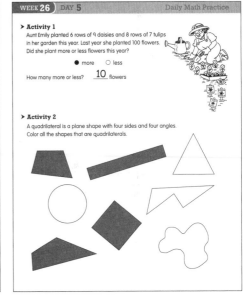

**WEEK 27 · DAY 5** — Daily Math Practice

> **Activity 1**
Look at the coins. Multiply each coin by the number next to it. Write the total value on the line.

   5 × ⊙ = $ __1.25__    3 × ⊙ = $ __1.50__    12 × ⊙ = $ __1.20__

   19 × ⊙ = $ __0.19__   12 × ⊙ = $ __0.60__

> **Activity 2**
How many products can you write in one minute?

   10     11     12     15     19     20     31
   × 2    × 3    × 4    × 2    × 1    × 3    × 0
   __20__ __33__ __48__ __30__ __19__ __60__ __0__

   11 × 6 = __66__    27 × 2 = __54__    4 × 12 = __48__    9 × 10 = __90__

   25     63     41     37     55     10     14
   × 2    × 3    × 4    × 5    × 2    × 8    × 3
   __50__ __189__ __164__ __185__ __110__ __80__ __42__

   ____ correct

## TE Page 88 / SB Page 82

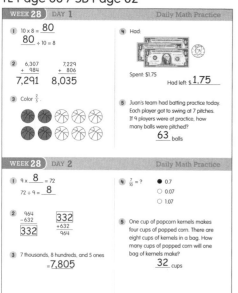

**WEEK 28 DAY 1** — Daily Math Practice

1. 10 × 8 = **80**
   **80** ÷ 10 = 8

2. 6,307   7,229
   + 984   + 806
   **7,291**  **8,035**

3. Color 2/5

4. Had:
   Spent: $1.75
   Had left: $ **1.75**

5. Juan's team had batting practice today. Each player got to swing at 7 pitches. If 9 players were at practice, how many balls were pitched?
   **63** balls

**WEEK 28 DAY 2** — Daily Math Practice

1. 9 × **8** = 72
   72 ÷ 9 = **8**

2. 964      **332**
   − 632    + 632
   **332**    964

3. 7 thousands, 8 hundreds, and 5 ones
   = **7,805**

4. 7/10 = ?   ● 0.7  ○ 0.07  ○ 1.07

5. One cup of popcorn kernels makes four cups of popped corn. There are eight cups of kernels in a bag. How many cups of kernels corn will one bag of kernels make?
   **32** cups

## TE Page 89 / SB Page 83

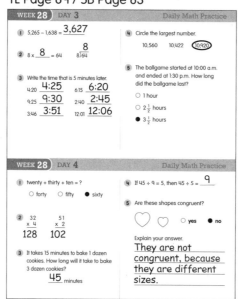

**WEEK 28 DAY 3** — Daily Math Practice

1. 5,265 − 1,638 = **3,627**

2. 8 × **8** = 64    **8**
                    8)64

3. Write the time that is 5 minutes later.
   4:20 **4:25**   6:15 **6:20**
   9:25 **9:30**   2:40 **2:45**
   3:46 **3:51**   12:01 **12:06**

4. Circle the largest number.
   10,560   10,422   (10,920)

5. The ballgame started at 10:00 a.m. and ended at 1:30 p.m. How long did the ballgame last?
   ○ 1 hour
   ○ 2½ hours
   ● 3½ hours

**WEEK 28 DAY 4** — Daily Math Practice

1. twenty + thirty + ten = ?
   ○ forty  ○ fifty  ● sixty

2. 32      51
   × 4     × 2
   **128**   **102**

3. It takes 15 minutes to bake 1 dozen cookies. How long will it take to bake 3 dozen cookies?
   **45** minutes

4. If 45 ÷ 9 = 5, then 45 ÷ 5 = **9**

5. Are these shapes congruent?
   ○ yes  ● no
   Explain your answer.
   **They are not congruent, because they are different sizes.**

## TE Page 90 / SB Page 84

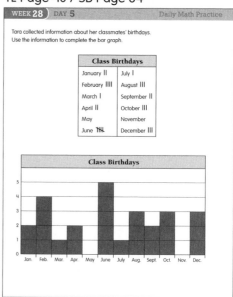

**WEEK 28 DAY 5** — Daily Math Practice

Tara collected information about her classmates' birthdays. Use the information to complete the bar graph.

| Class Birthdays | |
|---|---|
| January II | July I |
| February IIII | August III |
| March I | September II |
| April II | October III |
| May | November |
| June IIII | December III |

**Class Birthdays** (bar graph)

## TE Page 91 / SB Page 85

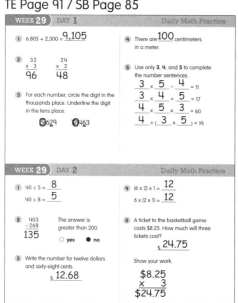

**WEEK 29 DAY 1** — Daily Math Practice

1. 6,805 + 2,300 = **9,105**

2. 32      24
   × 3     × 2
   **96**    **48**

3. For each number, circle the digit in the thousands place. Underline the digit in the tens place.
   5,629   12,463

4. There are **100** centimeters in a meter.

5. Use only 3, 4, and 5 to complete the number sentences.
   **3** × **5** − **4** = 11
   **3** × **4** + **5** = 17
   **4** × **5** × **3** = 60
   **4** + ( **3** × **5** ) = 19

**WEEK 29 DAY 2** — Daily Math Practice

1. 40 ÷ 5 = **8**
   40 ÷ 8 = **5**

2. 403
   − 268
   **135**
   The answer is greater than 200.
   ○ yes  ● no

3. Write the number for twelve dollars and sixty-eight cents.
   $ **12.68**

4. (6 × 2) × 1 = **12**
   6 × (2 × 1) = **12**

5. A ticket to the basketball game costs $8.25. How much will three tickets cost?
   $ **24.75**
   Show your work.
   $8.25
   × 3
   $24.75

## TE Page 92 / SB Page 86

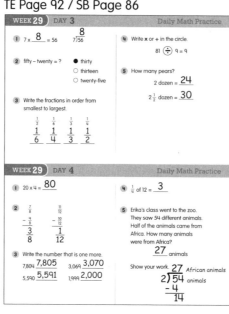

**WEEK 29 DAY 3** — Daily Math Practice

1. 7 × **8** = 56    **8**
                    7)56

2. fifty − twenty = ?
   ● thirty  ○ thirteen  ○ twenty-five

3. Write the fractions in order from smallest to largest.
   1/2   1/4   1/3   1/6
   **1/6   1/4   1/3   1/2**

4. Write x or + in the circle.
   81 ÷ 9 = 9

5. How many pears?
   2 dozen = **24**
   2½ dozen = **30**

**WEEK 29 DAY 4** — Daily Math Practice

1. 20 × 4 = **80**

2. 7/8      11/12
   − 4/8    − 10/12
   **3/8**    **1/12**

3. Write the number that is one more.
   7,804 **7,805**   3,069 **3,070**
   5,590 **5,591**   1,999 **2,000**

4. 1/4 of 12 = **3**

5. Erika's class went to the zoo. They saw 54 different animals. Half of the animals came from Africa. How many animals were from Africa?
   **27** animals
   Show your work. **27** African animals
   27
   2)54 animals
   − 4
   14

## TE Page 93 / SB Page 87

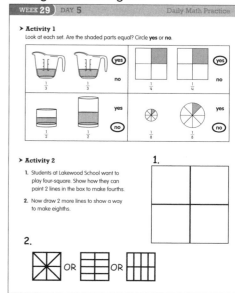

**WEEK 29 DAY 5** — Daily Math Practice

**Activity 1**
Look at each set. Are the shaded parts equal? Circle **yes** or **no**.

(yes / no) 1/3 1/3 — yes
(yes / no) 1/4 1/4 — no
1/2 1/2 — yes
1/8 — yes/no

**Activity 2**
1. Students at Lakewood School want to play four-square. Show how they can paint 2 lines in the box to make fourths.
2. Now draw 2 more lines to show a way to make eighths.

1.
2. [grid] OR [grid] OR [grid]

## TE Page 94 / SB Page 88

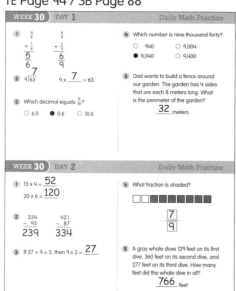

**WEEK 30 DAY 1** — Daily Math Practice

1. 4/6        4/9
   + 1/6      + 2/9
   **5/6**      **6/9**

2. **7**           9 × **7** = 63
   9)63

3. Which decimal equals 6/10?
   ○ 6.0  ● 0.6  ○ 10.6

4. Which number is nine thousand forty?
   ○ 940   ○ 9,004
   ● 9,040   ○ 9,400

5. Dad wants to build a fence around our garden. The garden has 4 sides that are each 8 meters long. What is the perimeter of the garden?
   **32** meters

**WEEK 30 DAY 2** — Daily Math Practice

1. 13 × 4 = **52**
   20 × 6 = **120**

2. 334       421
   − 95      − 87
   **239**     **334**

3. If 27 ÷ 9 = 3, then 9 × 3 = **27**

4. What fraction is shaded?
   **7/9**

5. A gray whale dove 129 feet on its first dive, 360 feet on its second dive, and 277 feet on its third dive. How many feet did the whale dive in all?
   **766** feet

## TE Page 95 / SB Page 89

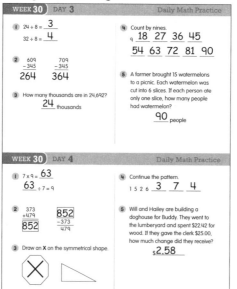

**WEEK 30 DAY 3** — Daily Math Practice

1. 24 ÷ 8 = **3**
   32 ÷ 8 = **4**

2. 609       709
   − 345     − 345
   **264**     **364**

3. How many thousands are in 24,692?
   **24** thousands

4. Count by nines.
   9 **18 27 36 45**
   **54 63 72 81 90**

5. A farmer brought 15 watermelons to a picnic. Each watermelon was cut into 6 slices. If each person ate only one slice, how many people had watermelon?
   **90** people

**WEEK 30 DAY 4** — Daily Math Practice

1. 7 × 9 = **63**
   **63** ÷ 7 = 9

2. 373       **852**
   + 479     − 373
   **852**     479

3. Draw an X on the symmetrical shape.

4. Continue the pattern.
   1 5 2 6 **3 7 4**

5. Will and Hailey are building a doghouse for Buddy. They went to the lumberyard and spent $22.42 for wood. If they gave the clerk $25.00, how much change did they receive?
   $ **2.58**

## TE Page 96 / SB Page 90

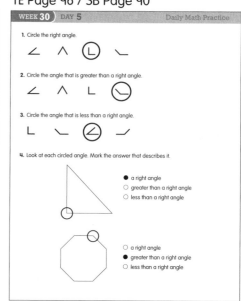

**WEEK 30 DAY 5** — Daily Math Practice

1. Circle the right angle.

2. Circle the angle that is greater than a right angle.

3. Circle the angle that is less than a right angle.

4. Look at each circled angle. Mark the answer that describes it.
   ● a right angle
   ○ greater than a right angle
   ○ less than a right angle

   ○ a right angle
   ● greater than a right angle
   ○ less than a right angle

## TE Page 97 / SB Page 91

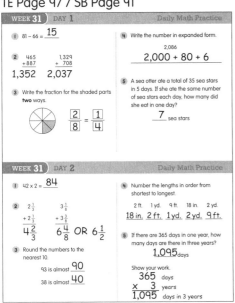

**WEEK 31 · DAY 1** — Daily Math Practice

1. 81 − 66 = __15__

2. 465 + 887 = __1,352__   1,329 + 708 = __2,037__

3. Write the fraction for the shaded parts **two** ways.
$$\frac{2}{8} = \frac{1}{4}$$

4. Write the number in expanded form.
2,086
__2,000 + 80 + 6__

5. A sea otter ate a total of 35 sea stars in 5 days. If she ate the same number of sea stars each day, how many did she eat in one day?
__7__ sea stars

**WEEK 31 · DAY 2** — Daily Math Practice

1. 42 × 2 = __84__

2. $2\frac{1}{3} + 2\frac{1}{3} = 4\frac{2}{3}$   $3\frac{1}{8} + 3\frac{3}{8} = 6\frac{4}{8}$ OR $6\frac{1}{2}$

3. Round the numbers to the nearest 10.
93 is almost __90__
38 is almost __40__

4. Number the lengths in order from shortest to longest.
2 ft.   1 yd.   9 ft.   18 in.   2 yd.
__18 in.__  __2 ft.__  __1 yd.__  __2 yd.__  __9 ft.__

5. If there are 365 days in one year, how many days are there in three years?
__1,095__ days

Show your work.
365 days
× 3 years
__1,095__ days in 3 years

## TE Page 98 / SB Page 92

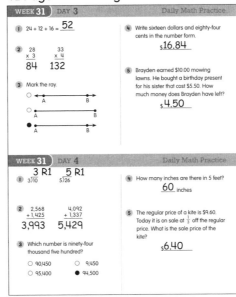

**WEEK 31 · DAY 3** — Daily Math Practice

1. 24 + 12 + 16 = __52__

2. 28 × 3 = __84__   33 × 4 = __132__

3. Mark the ray.
○ A ↔ B
○ A — B
● A → B

4. Write sixteen dollars and eighty-four cents in the number form.
$__16.84__

5. Brayden earned $10.00 mowing lawns. He bought a birthday present for his sister that cost $5.50. How much money does Brayden have left?
$__4.50__

**WEEK 31 · DAY 4** — Daily Math Practice

1. 3)10 = __3 R1__   5)26 = __5 R1__

2. 2,568 + 1,425 = __3,993__   4,092 + 1,337 = __5,429__

3. Which number is ninety-four thousand five hundred?
○ 90,450   ○ 9,450
○ 95,400   ● 94,500

4. How many inches are there in 5 feet?
__60__ inches

5. The regular price of a kite is $9.60. Today it is on sale $\frac{1}{3}$ off the regular price. What is the sale price of the kite?
$__6.40__

## TE Page 99 / SB Page 93

**WEEK 31 · DAY 5** — Daily Math Practice

**Activity 1**
Write the equivalent fraction and decimal for each amount.

| Amount | Fraction | Decimal |
|---|---|---|
| 4 cents | $\frac{4}{100}$ | $0.04 |
| 12 cents | $\frac{12}{100}$ | $0.12 |
| 25 cents | $\frac{25}{100}$ | $0.25 |
| 50 cents | $\frac{50}{100}$ | $0.50 |
| 100 cents | $\frac{100}{100}$ | $1.00 |

**Activity 2**
1. How many quotients can you write in one minute?
5)25 = __5__   9)18 = __2__   3)21 = __7__   4)32 = __8__   9)81 = __9__
60 ÷ 6 = __10__   40 ÷ 5 = __8__   90 ÷ 10 = __9__

2. Solve with remainders.
5)11 = __2 R1__   6)43 = __7 R1__   5)51 = __10 R1__   8)66 = __8 R2__   7)55 = __7 R6__

_____ correct

## TE Page 100 / SB Page 94

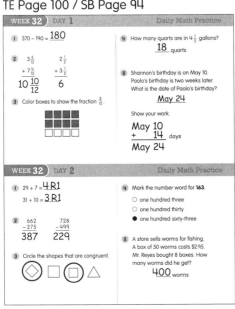

**WEEK 32 · DAY 1** — Daily Math Practice

1. 370 − 190 = __180__

2. $3\frac{5}{12} + 7\frac{5}{12} = 10\frac{10}{12}$   $2\frac{1}{2} + 3\frac{1}{2} = 6$

3. Color boxes to show the fraction $\frac{8}{12}$.

4. How many quarts are in $4\frac{1}{2}$ gallons?
__18__ quarts

5. Shannon's birthday is on May 10. Paolo's birthday is two weeks later. What is the date of Paolo's birthday?
__May 24__

Show your work.
May 10
+ 14 days
May 24

**WEEK 32 · DAY 2** — Daily Math Practice

1. 29 ÷ 7 = __4 R1__
31 ÷ 10 = __3 R1__

2. 662 − 275 = __387__   728 − 499 = __229__

3. Circle the shapes that are congruent.

4. Mark the number word for **163**.
○ one hundred three
○ one hundred thirty
● one hundred sixty-three

5. A store sells worms for fishing. A box of 50 worms costs $2.95. Mr. Reyes bought 8 boxes. How many worms did he get?
__400__ worms

## TE Page 101 / SB Page 95

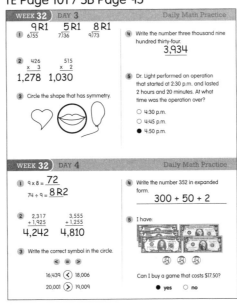

**WEEK 32 · DAY 3** — Daily Math Practice

1. 6)55 = __9 R1__   7)36 = __5 R1__   9)73 = __8 R1__

2. 426 × 3 = __1,278__   515 × 2 = __1,030__

3. Circle the shape that has symmetry.

4. Write the number three thousand nine hundred thirty-four.
__3,934__

5. Dr. Light performed an operation that started at 2:30 p.m. and lasted 2 hours and 20 minutes. At what time was the operation over?
○ 4:30 p.m.
○ 4:45 p.m.
● 4:50 p.m.

**WEEK 32 · DAY 4** — Daily Math Practice

1. 9 × 8 = __72__
74 ÷ 9 = __8 R2__

2. 2,317 + 1,925 = __4,242__   3,555 + 1,255 = __4,810__

3. Write the correct symbol in the circle.
16,439 ( < ) 18,006
20,001 ( > ) 19,009

4. Write the number 352 in expanded form.
__300 + 50 + 2__

5. I have:

Can I buy a game that costs $17.50?
● yes   ○ no

## TE Page 102 / SB Page 96

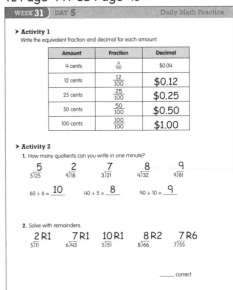

**WEEK 32 · DAY 5** — Daily Math Practice

**Activity 1**
Sara is making individual fruit salads for the 6 people in her family. Each salad will have 3 apple slices, 6 banana chunks, 2 orange wedges, and 5 grapes. How many pieces of fruit will Sara prepare for all of the salads?
__96__ pieces of fruit

Show your work.
18 apple slices + 36 banana chunks = 54
54 + 12 orange wedges = 66
66 + 30 grapes = 96 pieces of fruit

**Activity 2**
Two of the numbers below have a sum of 10 and a product of 24.
2  3  4  5  6

What are the numbers? __6__ and __4__

Show your work.
4 + 6 = 10
6 × 4 = 24

## TE Page 103 / SB Page 97

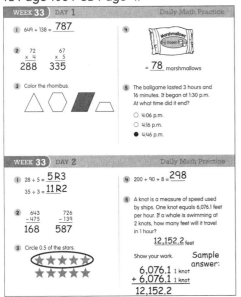

**WEEK 33 · DAY 1** — Daily Math Practice

1. 649 + 138 = __787__

2. 72 × 4 = __288__   67 × 5 = __335__

3. Color the rhombus.

4. __= 78__ marshmallows

5. The ballgame lasted 3 hours and 16 minutes. It began at 1:30 p.m. At what time did it end?
○ 4:06 p.m.
○ 4:16 p.m.
● 4:46 p.m.

**WEEK 33 · DAY 2** — Daily Math Practice

1. 28 ÷ 5 = __5 R3__
35 ÷ 3 = __11 R2__

2. 643 − 475 = __168__   726 − 139 = __587__

3. Circle 0.5 of the stars.

4. 200 + 90 + 8 = __298__

5. A knot is a measure of speed used by ships. One knot equals 6,076.1 feet per hour. If a whale is swimming at 2 knots, how many feet will it travel in 1 hour?
__12,152.2__ feet

Show your work.   Sample answer:
6,076.1 1 knot
+ 6,076.1 1 knot
12,152.2

## TE Page 104 / SB Page 98

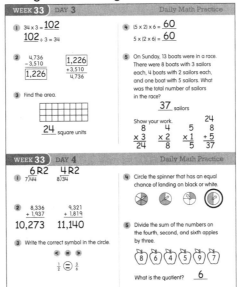

**WEEK 33 · DAY 3** — Daily Math Practice

1. 34 × 3 = __102__
__102__ ÷ 3 = 34

2. 4,736 − 3,510 = __1,226__
1,226 + 3,510 = 4,736

3. Find the area.
__24__ square units

4. (5 × 2) × 6 = __60__
5 × (2 × 6) = __60__

5. On Sunday, 13 boats were in a race. There were 8 boats with 3 sailors each, 4 boats with 2 sailors each, and one boat with 5 sailors. What was the total number of sailors in the race?
__37__ sailors

Show your work.
8 × 3 = 24   4 × 2 = 8   5 × 1 = 5   24 + 5 = ... + 5 = 37

**WEEK 33 · DAY 4** — Daily Math Practice

1. 7)44 = __6 R2__   8)34 = __4 R2__

2. 8,336 + 1,937 = __10,273__   9,321 + 1,819 = __11,140__

3. Write the correct symbol in the circle.
$\frac{1}{2}$ ( = ) $\frac{3}{6}$

4. Circle the spinner that has an equal chance of landing on black or white.

5. Divide the sum of the numbers on the fourth, second, and sixth apples by three.
8  4  6  8
What is the quotient? __6__

## TE Page 105 / SB Page 99

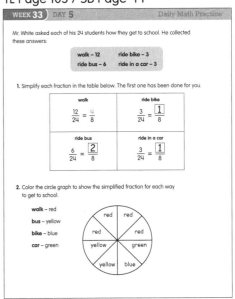

**WEEK 33 · DAY 5** — Daily Math Practice

Mr. White asked each of his 24 students how they get to school. He collected these answers:

walk – 12   ride bike – 3
ride bus – 6   ride in a car – 3

1. Simplify each fraction in the table below. The first one has been done for you.

| walk | ride bike |
|---|---|
| $\frac{12}{24} = \frac{4}{8}$ | $\frac{3}{24} = \frac{1}{8}$ |

| ride bus | ride in a car |
|---|---|
| $\frac{6}{24} = \frac{2}{8}$ | $\frac{3}{24} = \frac{1}{8}$ |

2. Color the circle graph to show the simplified fraction for each way to get to school.

walk – red
bus – yellow
bike – blue
car – green

## TE Page 106 / SB Page 100

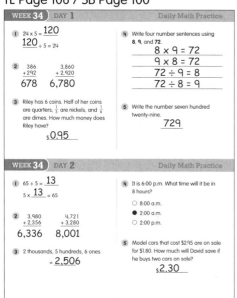

**WEEK 34　DAY 1**　Daily Math Practice

1. 24 x 5 = **120**
   **120** ÷ 5 = 24

2. 386   3,860
   +292  +2,920
   **678**  **6,780**

3. Riley has 6 coins. Half of her coins are quarters, ⅓ are nickels, and ⅙ are dimes. How much money does Riley have?
   $**0.95**

4. Write four number sentences using **8, 9,** and **72**.
   **8 x 9 = 72**
   **9 x 8 = 72**
   **72 ÷ 9 = 8**
   **72 ÷ 8 = 9**

5. Write the number seven hundred twenty-nine.
   **729**

**WEEK 34　DAY 2**

1. 65 ÷ 5 = **13**
   5 x **13** = 65

2. 3,980   4,721
   +2,356  +3,280
   **6,336**  **8,001**

3. 2 thousands, 5 hundreds, 6 ones
   = **2,506**

4. It is 6:00 p.m. What time will it be in 8 hours?
   ○ 8:00 a.m.
   ● 2:00 a.m.
   ○ 2:00 p.m.

5. Model cars that cost $2.95 are on sale for $1.80. How much will David save if he buys two cars on sale?
   $**2.30**

## TE Page 107 / SB Page 101

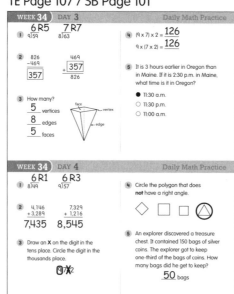

**WEEK 34　DAY 3**　Daily Math Practice

1. **6 R5**      **7 R7**
   9)59        8)63

2. 826       469
   −469     +**357**
   **357**     826

3. How many?
   **5** vertices
   **8** edges
   **5** faces

4. (9 x 7) x 2 = **126**
   9 x (7 x 2) = **126**

5. It is 3 hours earlier in Oregon than in Maine. If it is 2:30 p.m. in Maine, what time is it in Oregon?
   ● 11:30 a.m.
   ○ 11:30 p.m.
   ○ 11:00 a.m.

**WEEK 34　DAY 4**

1. **6 R1**      **6 R3**
   8)49        9)57

2. 4,146   7,329
   +3,289  +1,216
   **7,435**  **8,545**

3. Draw an **X** on the digit in the tens place. Circle the digit in the thousands place.
   ⑨7🅇2

4. Circle the polygon that does **not** have a right angle.
   ◇ □ ▢ △

5. An explorer discovered a treasure chest. It contained 150 bags of silver coins. The explorer got to keep one-third of the bags of coins. How many bags did he get to keep?
   **50** bags

## TE Page 108 / SB Page 102

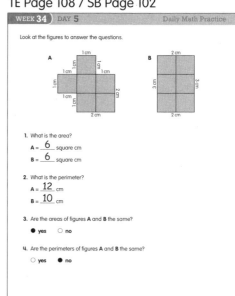

**WEEK 34　DAY 5**　Daily Math Practice

Look at the figures to answer the questions.

1. What is the area?
   A = **6** square cm
   B = **6** square cm

2. What is the perimeter?
   A = **12** cm
   B = **10** cm

3. Are the areas of figures **A** and **B** the same?
   ● yes　○ no

4. Are the perimeters of figures **A** and **B** the same?
   ○ yes　● no

## TE Page 109 / SB Page 103

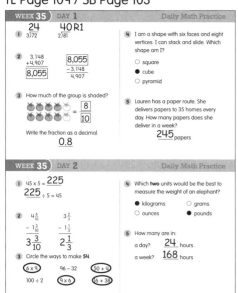

**WEEK 35　DAY 1**　Daily Math Practice

1. **24**       **40 R1**
   3)72       2)81

2. 3,148     **8,055**
   +4,907   − 3,148
   **8,055**     4,907

3. How much of the group is shaded?
   = **8/10**
   Write the fraction as a decimal.
   **0.8**

4. I am a shape with six faces and eight vertices. I can stack and slide. Which shape am I?
   ○ square
   ● cube
   ○ pyramid

5. Lauren has a paper route. She delivers papers to 35 homes every day. How many papers does she deliver in a week?
   **245** papers

**WEEK 35　DAY 2**

1. 45 x 5 = **225**
   **225** ÷ 5 = 45

2. 4 6/10    3 2/3
   − 1 3/10   − 1 1/3
   **3 3/10**    **2 1/3**

3. Circle the ways to make 54.
   (6 x 9)    96 − 32    (50 + 4)
   100 ÷ 2   (9 x 6)    (16 + 38)

4. Which **two** units would be the best to measure the weight of an elephant?
   ● kilograms　○ grams
   ○ ounces　● pounds

5. How many are in:
   a day? **24** hours
   a week? **168** hours

## TE Page 110 / SB Page 104

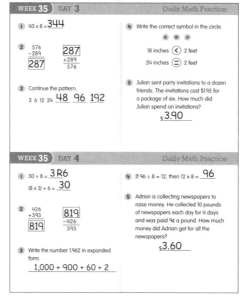

**WEEK 35　DAY 3**　Daily Math Practice

1. 43 x 8 = **344**

2. 576      **287**
   −289    +289
   **287**     576

3. Continue the pattern.
   3 6 12 24 **48  96  192**

4. Write the correct symbol in the circle.
   < = >
   18 inches ⓛ 2 feet
   24 inches ⓔ 2 feet

5. Julian sent party invitations to a dozen friends. The invitations cost $1.95 for a package of six. How much did Julian spend on invitations?
   $**3.90**

**WEEK 35　DAY 4**

1. 30 ÷ 8 = **3 R6**
   (8 x 3) + 6 = **30**

2. 426      **819**
   +393    −426
   **819**     393

3. Write the number 1,962 in expanded form.
   **1,000 + 900 + 60 + 2**

4. If 96 ÷ 8 = 12, then 12 x 8 = **96**

5. Adrian is collecting newspapers to raise money. He collected 10 pounds of newspapers each day for 4 days and was paid 9¢ a pound. How much money did Adrian get for all the newspapers?
   $**3.60**

## TE Page 111 / SB Page 105

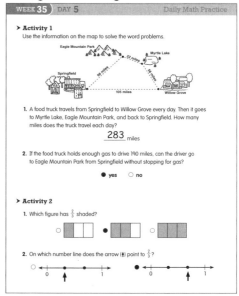

**WEEK 35　DAY 5**　Daily Math Practice

➤ **Activity 1**
Use the information on the map to solve the word problems.

1. A food truck travels from Springfield to Willow Grove every day. Then it goes to Myrtle Lake, Eagle Mountain Park, and back to Springfield. How many miles does the truck travel each day?
   **283** miles

2. If the food truck holds enough gas to drive 190 miles, can the driver go to Eagle Mountain Park from Springfield without stopping for gas?
   ● yes　○ no

➤ **Activity 2**

1. Which figure has ⅔ shaded?

2. On which number line does the arrow (↑) point to ⅔?

## TE Page 112 / SB Page 106

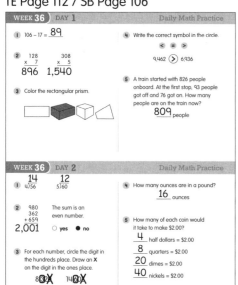

**WEEK 36　DAY 1**　Daily Math Practice

1. 106 − 17 = **89**

2. 128      308
   x 7      x 5
   **896**     **1,540**

3. Color the rectangular prism.

4. Write the correct symbol in the circle.
   < = >
   9,462 (>) 6,936

5. A train started with 826 people onboard. At the first stop, 93 people got off and 76 got on. How many people are on the train now?
   **809** people

**WEEK 36　DAY 2**

1. **14**       **12**
   4)56       5)60

2. 980      The sum is an
   362      even number.
   +659
   **2,001**    ○ yes ● no

3. For each number, circle the digit in the hundreds place. Draw an **X** on the digit in the ones place.
   8🅇3🅇    14🅇0🅇

4. How many ounces are in a pound?
   **16** ounces

5. How many of each coin would it take to make $2.00?
   **4** half dollars = $2.00
   **8** quarters = $2.00
   **20** dimes = $2.00
   **40** nickels = $2.00

## TE Page 113 / SB Page 107

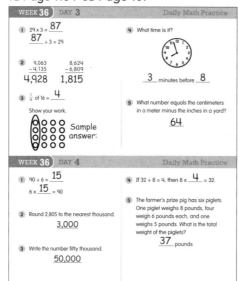

**WEEK 36　DAY 3**　Daily Math Practice

1. 29 x 3 = **87**
   **87** ÷ 3 = 29

2. 9,063    8,624
   −4,135   − 6,809
   **4,928**    **1,815**

3. ¼ of 16 = **4**
   Show your work.
   Sample answer:

4. What time is it?
   **3** minutes before **8**

5. What number equals the centimeters in a meter minus the inches in a yard?
   **64**

**WEEK 36　DAY 4**

1. 90 ÷ 6 = **15**
   6 x **15** = 90

2. Round 2,805 to the nearest thousand.
   **3,000**

3. Write the number fifty thousand.
   **50,000**

4. If 32 ÷ 8 = 4, then 8 x **4** = 32.

5. The farmer's prize pig has six piglets. One piglet weighs 8 pounds, four weigh 6 pounds each, and one weighs 5 pounds. What is the total weight of the piglets?
   **37** pounds

## TE Page 114 / SB Page 108

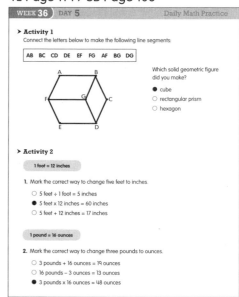

**WEEK 36　DAY 5**　Daily Math Practice

➤ **Activity 1**
Connect the letters below to make the following line segments:

AB  BC  CD  DE  EF  FG  AF  BG  DG

Which solid geometric figure did you make?
● cube
○ rectangular prism
○ hexagon

➤ **Activity 2**

| 1 foot = 12 inches |

1. Mark the correct way to change five feet to inches.
   ○ 5 feet ÷ 1 foot = 5 inches
   ● 5 feet x 12 inches = 60 inches
   ○ 5 feet + 12 inches = 17 inches

| 1 pound = 16 ounces |

2. Mark the correct way to change three pounds to ounces.
   ○ 3 pounds + 16 ounces = 19 ounces
   ○ 16 pounds − 3 ounces = 13 ounces
   ● 3 pounds x 16 ounces = 48 ounces

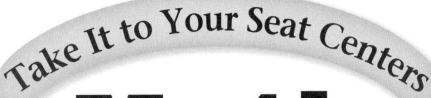

# Take It to Your Seat Centers

# Math

## Grades K-6

## Independent practice, perfect for students at all levels.

## Take It to Your Seat Centers: Math

Hands-on practice of core math skills! Each of the 12 centers focuses on key math concepts and presents skill practice in engaging visual and tactile activities. The easy-to-assemble centers include full-color cards and mats, directions, answer keys, and student record forms. Ideal for any classroom and to support RTI or ELLs. 160 full-color pages. Correlated to current standards.

**www.evan-moor.com/tmcent**

| | Teacher's Edition Print | | Teacher's Edition E-book |
|---|---|---|---|
| GRADE | EMC | GRADE | EMC |
| K | 3070 | K | 3070i |
| 1 | 3071 | 1 | 3071i |
| 2 | 3072 | 2 | 3072i |
| 3 | 3073 | 3 | 3073i |
| 4 | 3074 | 4 | 3074i |
| 5 | 3075 | 5 | 3075i |
| 6 | 3076 | 6 | 3076i |

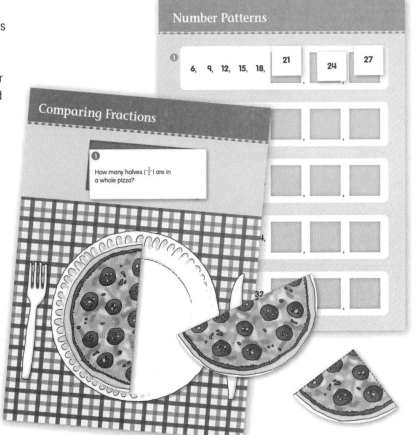

# Daily Language Review

## Improve language skills and vocabulary with *Daily Language Review*!

Students practice grammar, punctuation, usage, and sentence-editing skills using the research-based model of frequent, focused practice.

Rigorous practice of conventions of standard English skills.

The concise daily lessons engage students as they practice standards-aligned language skills.

Includes a detailed scope and sequence, skills list, and home–school connection projects.

*Correlated to current standards*

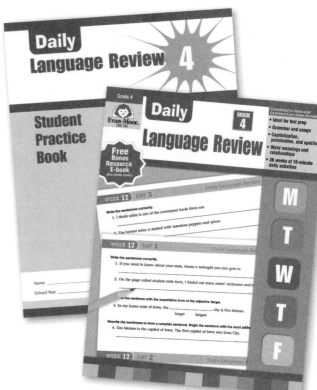

| Teacher's Edition* | | Student Pack (5 Student Books) | |
|---|---|---|---|
| Grade 1 | EMC 579 | Grade 1 | EMC 6515 |
| Grade 2 | EMC 580 | Grade 2 | EMC 6516 |
| Grade 3 | EMC 581 | Grade 3 | EMC 6517 |
| Grade 4 | EMC 582 | Grade 4 | EMC 6518 |
| Grade 5 | EMC 583 | Grade 5 | EMC 6519 |
| Grade 6 | EMC 576 | Grade 6 | EMC 6520 |
| Grade 7 | EMC 2797 | Grade 7 | EMC 6597 |
| Grade 8 | EMC 2798 | Grade 8 | EMC 6598 |

*Available in print and e-book*

*"I used **Daily Language Review** as a weekly homework assignment with my students. It was amazing to see how much they improved from the beginning of the year to the end. I'm definitely going to incorporate it again this year. Thank you for a great product!"*

Fourth Grade Teacher, California